MEETI

Meeting God in Every Moment

The Art of Living in God's Presence

David E. Rosage

SERVANT BOOKS
Ann Arbor, Michigan

Copyright © 1987 by David E. Rosage
All rights reserved.

Scripture texts used in this work are taken from the NEW
AMERICAN BIBLE, Copyright © 1970 by the Confraternity
of Christian Doctrine, Washington, D.C. and are used by
license of said copyright owner. No part of the NEW
AMERICAN BIBLE may be reproduced in any form without
permission in writing. All rights reserved.

Published by Servant Books
P.O. Box 8617
Ann Arbor, Michigan 48107

Cover design by Michael P. Andaloro
Cover photograph by Anthony A. Boccaccio/The Image Bank

Printed in the United States of America
ISBN 0-89283-319-X

87 88 89 90 91 10 9 8 7 6 5 4 3 2 1

Dedicated to
Mothers, Fathers, Teachers,
and
Everyone Who Helped Us Discover

Contents

Introduction

Journey with me among the ordinary happenings of daily life to discover what I call the "mystery in the mundane." God is present in all of his creation—sustaining, energizing, re-creating. His mysterious presence surrounds us, envelops us, possesses us, and fills us with his love.

We are easily aware of the majesty and might of God when we see a towering, snow-capped mountain. Likewise an expansive blue sky raises our hearts to praise and glorify our creative Father, and our delight overflows at his beauty in a beautiful, ever-changing sunset.

This same mighty God does not so easily capture our attention nor stimulate our reflection in the ordinary happenings of our busy, workaday world. It requires some effort to rivet our attention and reflect upon an insignificant object, to allow its meaning to penetrate our mind until it reaches our heart.

God's handiwork in creation is the window through which we encounter him. We must routinely pause to experience his presence and power with the eyes of faith. Only then only will eyesight generate insight.

Formal prayer does not always sustain us amid the demanding preoccupations of every day. If we strive to keep ourselves more aware of God's presence in the ordinary, then we will find ourselves maturing more rapidly in our spiritual development.

These encounters with God are not for a few privileged people. On the contrary, the Lord wishes every one of us to walk in his abiding presence. Did he not promise, "Know that I am with you always, until the end of the world" (Mt 28:20)? Recognizing the "mystery in the mundane" will help us maintain an attitude of prayer even as daily preoccupations crowd in on us. Because there are fifty-two meditations, you may want to use the book throughout an entire year, focusing on one meditation each week.

This truth was impressed upon me rather forcefully by a brief film clip I saw recently. A woman dressed rather elegantly was making her way to daily Mass, carrying her large prayer book. As she proceeded down the sidewalk, a newsboy asked if she would like a morning paper. She dismissed him with a wordless frown, nearly a scowl. Continuing her walk, she made no attempt to respond to the bus driver's cheery "Good morning." On reaching the church, she encountered the janitor, who doffed his cap and with grimy hands held the door open for her. His gentlemanly gesture was totally ignored. The script of this film clip was only one sentence: "If you haven't found him in them, you won't find him in there."

The Lord is equally present in the earthly as in the heavenly, in the ordinary as in the magnificent. This book is a collection of life's ordinary experiences. May they encourage us to stop, look, and listen more frequently and more reflectively to the Lord's "still small voice."

My hope is that they will help us hear the Lord throughout our whole day.

Part I

People

ONE

People Are Like Books

My wanderings . . . are they not recorded in your book?
(Ps 56:9)

In the new section of the ancient city of Jerusalem, there is a famous museum known as the Shrine of the Book. In its safekeeping are many ancient and valuable manuscripts, including the Dead Sea Scrolls. The literature and lore of this museum are priceless.

In its own way every book is a shrine. Books supply us with valuable information. They offer us enjoyment, enlightenment, and encouragement. They may take us on a pleasant journey to a distant land or acquaint us with treasures close to home. A book is made up of many pages, each one revealing something new and different.

People are like books. Each of our daily experiences adds another page to who we are. Some of these experiences are delightful, others exciting, some sad. Each year adds another chapter.

A book is written for a definite purpose, and it is meant to bear some particular fruit. The pages of our book of life all point to a happy ending with our Father in heaven. The Lord remembers our good deeds and keeps them in his book, as the psalmist reminds us:

My wanderings you have counted;
my tears are stored in your flask;
are they not recorded in your book? (Ps 56:9)

Some home libraries display books, even whole sets, that are attractively bound and neatly arranged on a

3

shelf. For the most part they are unfingered and unread for long periods of time, but they do convey an impression of culture and scholarship. Similarly, some people present an attractive appearance. They are elegantly dressed, properly poised, and even quite well-informed. But they are little used because they keep themselves aloof from the warp and woof of daily living. Like a decorative set of books, they remain on the shelf.

Some libraries contain learned tomes laden with information, but they divulge this information only if studied and restudied. So too the human race boasts people who are wellsprings of information but do not share their wealth of learning very readily. They may be reserved or sophisticated, or simply reluctant to be bothered with the affairs of life.

We have all seen and most of us possess books that are dog-eared and well-thumbed. These books have given much enjoyment to many readers. Perhaps we ourselves have read and reread some of them on occasion. They seem to have an attractive personality. They are at our beck and call and meet our many needs. Such books as the Bible, our prayer book, a favorite cookbook, and even the dictionary come to mind immediately. These books remind me of people I know. They are always available. They are eager and anxious to give whenever asked. They are always at hand when I need them.

People are like books. Some are humorous and entertaining, keeping our hearts lightsome and filling us with joy. Some are inspirational and uplifting, raising our minds and hearts to higher things and giving us a deeper appreciation of the niceties of life. Some are mystery stories, and we never know what is going on inside them. Others are instructional, leading us into a new understanding of our unexplored worlds and life's experiences.

Then there is the *the Book*, the Bible, God's book. *Bible* in Greek simply means "the Book"; no other title or designation is necessary.

In his book God shares himself. He tells us how precious we are to him and how much he loves us. He is deeply concerned about us, his children.

Jesus came as the Word of God. He reveals himself in his written word. We get to know him as a gentle, loving Lord as we peruse his book, the New Testament. This kind of knowledge helps us establish an intimate, personal bond with him.

No book can contain Jesus. John says, "There are still many other things that Jesus did, yet if they were written about in detail, I doubt there would be room enough in the entire world to hold the books to record them" (Jn 21:25).

TWO

Bellhop, Please

"When you call me . . . I will listen to you." (Jer 29:12)

We are a mobile society. Many of us travel extensively throughout our beautiful country and even to other lands. We often encounter bellhops, those wonderful hotel employees who escort guests to their rooms, assist them with their luggage, and run errands.

The proper bellhop is neatly uniformed for immediate recognition. He is hospitable, showing concern for the visitor's well-being and standing by, ready to serve our every need. All of this concern and service comes with a price, of course. Even though bellhops are gainfully employed, the patron is expected to chip in his or her fair share.

On one of my trips my luggage did not catch the same plane I did. I arrived at the hotel quite late, so I advised the bellhop to keep my luggage when it arrived. I would call for it in the morning. Eager to be of assistance, however, the bellhop rang my bell at 2:30 a.m. with my luggage in tow. I think I thanked him and climbed back into bed.

The next morning as I crossed the lobby, the bellhop approached me to say that he was the one who had brought up my bags. Once again I thanked him, but he then mentioned that I had not tipped him. I apologized, reminding him that it had been 2:30 a.m., when I am not functioning too well.

I have the impression that some of us have developed a "bellhop" attitude toward our provident Father in heaven. We would like God to be a universal bellhop, whom we summon only when we are in need. Some of us have little time for God except when needs arise. When everything else fails, we urgently press him to come to our rescue or to grant a specific request. At times we are disappointed that he has not responded to our requests in the manner we had hoped.

We also betray a bellhop attitude toward our loving Father when we start bargaining with him. The service of a bellhop, we are well aware, requires a gratuity. This same mentality can creep into our relationship with God. We try to strike a bargain with him. We promise him that if this or that request is granted, we will do a certain thing for him.

God is our caring and concerned Father. He wants us to come to him in time of need. He awaits our petitions, but he also wants us to have the correct attitude of mind and heart. When we recognize our own inadequacy and our dependence upon him, he is very pleased. Jesus said it so plainly: "'Apart from me you can do nothing'" (Jn 15:5).

There is another side to the coin. God wants our praise and gratitude even more than our petitions. He is pleased at our willing acceptance of his will. Furthermore, he expects us to use his gifts and blessings for our own good and also for his honor and glory. When we do so, many of our prayers will be granted, some of them even before we ask them.

The Lord himself promised, "When you call me, when you go to pray to me, I will listen to you" (Jer 29:12).

THREE

Twofold Exercise

"Where two or three are gathered in my name, there am I in their midst." (Mt 18:20)

I have discovered that doctors almost to a person encourage some kind of regular physical exercise. Walking is high on their list of recommended exercises. However, there are many different kinds of walking. I distinguish between an exercise walk—in which we move rapidly, breathe deeply, and swing our arms freely—and one that is more contemplative.

A friend of mine says that he does not walk because it is too time-consuming. I have found that walking is by no means a waste of time. It is an ideal time to pray and be with the Lord. That's why I call it a prayer-exercise journey. Such a walk is conducive to our physical as well as our spiritual well-being.

First of all, while I walk I can thank the Lord that I am ambulatory. Some of my friends and acquaintances can no longer enjoy a brisk walk. Some are no longer able to walk more than a few steps. When I walk too far and my legs grow weary, I can still be grateful to the Lord and even apologize to him for neglecting to stay in shape.

If I walk too rapidly or up a steep grade, my huffing and puffing remind me to thank God for the invigorating oxygen and fresh air I enjoy as I breathe more than twenty-five thousand times each day. I can also thank him for permitting me to expel toxic gases and thus clear my bloodstream.

If I have a walking companion, an exercise walk can be very therapeutic as we share our daily experiences with one another. A couple who are dear friends of mine have found that walking is not only important but necessary. Speaking for Harry and herself, Kay writes: "Early in our marriage, we discovered that to communicate, to know and be known, meant taking time for each other. When the babies began to arrive— and there would be eight—we employed sitters. We would go for a walk or out for a Coke. We included babysitting expenses in a budget that hardly had enough to budget. This, I believe, was the beginning of our prayer. We shared our day, our feelings, our failures, and our hopes. When the children grew old enough for kitchen duty, we started going on walks after dinner. By the time we had five teenagers, I was most grateful that Harry and I had learned to share with each other, to share our burdens with the Lord, and to experience help and hope from both."

For Harry and Kay walking is by no means a waste of time. I wonder if Jesus did not have married couples in mind when he promised, "'If two of you join your voices on earth to pray for anything whatever, it shall be granted you by my Father in heaven. Where two or three are gathered in my name, there am I in their midst'" (Mt 18:19-20).

FOUR

Are We Patriotic People?

Let all your works give you thanks, O LORD. (Ps 145:10)

I was asked to give a talk at the luncheon meeting of a service organization. The topic assigned to me was "Are We Really Patriotic People?" My first impulse was to be very affirmative. Then I began to think more thoroughly about the subject.

As I reflected on this question, I began to realize that it is perhaps harder for us Americans to be patriotic than for some people whose homeland is centuries old. As a young nation, we have no long-standing traditions. We are made up of many different peoples who have found a haven here. We are a nation of many different cultures. People of older countries, such as Germany, Poland, or Ireland, have a more common background, with the same traditions and often the same religion. People of these countries can be more easily unified into a nation of one outlook. Patriotism flows from this kind of unity and oneness.

There are many reasons to be proud of America. We have always been generous to underdeveloped nations. Our foreign aid has gone to countries troubled by war and to the millions of hungry people throughout the world. God has blessed us with an abundance of his blessings, which we have shared generously with others. We have taken to heart the admonition of Jesus, "'Give, and it shall be given to you'" (Lk 6:38). We have also been motivated in our generosity by Jesus' words concerning the last judgment: "'I assure you, as often as you did it for one of my least brothers, you did it for me'" (Mt 25:40).

On the other hand, we can blush with shame at some

of the attitudes prevalent in our country. We do not recognize the sacredness of life as we ought. We have exploited our natural resources and polluted our air and waters for our own selfish gain, rather than being concerned about the common good and the generations who will follow in our footsteps.

Another sobering thought struck me as I was preparing my talk. History shows that many nations and cultures have been destroyed, not by an enemy alien, but from within, by the citizens who prefer their own selfish advantage to the welfare of the nation. Could this be happening in our beloved country?

As I pondered these thoughts, I was filled with gratitude to God for the countless blessings he has showered upon our country. His gifts are far too numerous for us to recall. I think immediately of the freedom we enjoy under our system of government, our rich natural resources, our fertile fields, our lakes, rivers, and waterways. Similar blessings number in the tens of thousands.

The psalmist often thanked God for his beneficence. I hear him say: "Let all your works give you thanks, O LORD, and let your faithful ones bless you. Let them discourse of the glory of your kingdom and speak of your might" (Ps 145:10-11).

FIVE

A Surprise Package

Her children rise up and praise her. (Prv 31:28)

One day the postman brought me a package that had been carefully wrapped, insured, and marked "Handle with Care." It was from my sister, but I did not have any idea what it was or why she had sent it. It was not Christmas, nor my birthday, nor any anniversary. However, sisters have a way of doing nice things even apart from any special occasion.

My curiosity aroused, I carefully unwrapped the outer paper, and with equal caution I removed the cushioned pad that protected the contents. By this time I could tell that it was a picture frame. I completed the unwrapping, and what a surprise! It was a picture of my mother, taken many years ago before her marriage. An old-fashioned frame complemented its antiquity.

My mother sat on a large log with hands resting in her lap. In her left hand she held a bunch of wild flowers, which she must have picked just before posing for this picture. She had a slight smile on her lips; her eyes, radiating peace and kindness, were looking directly at me.

With tear-filled eyes I sat down to admire this unexpected treasure. After sixty years I still miss Mother on occasion. There are many times when I would like to talk with her and discuss various decisions confronting me. I must admit that I still question God's plan in calling her to himself when I was only twelve years old and had four younger brothers and sisters.

I recall very vividly the Sunday afternoon when my mother was telling us that she had never felt better in her whole life. This was six months after giving birth to her sixth child. The following Thursday, at the age of 34, she was suddenly called to her heavenly reward.

All these years I have cherished one of my mother's final admonitions to me, given just a few days before she died. She must have suspected that she was soon to leave us. She told me that if she ever did leave her family, she was never going to abandon us. "If I should leave you," she said, "remember that you will always have two mothers. Remember, Jesus gave you his own mother as well as me. Now, what I want you to do is to come to both of us when you have a problem, or are perplexed about a decision, or face whatever else may come up in your life." Since this is what I considered my mother's dying wish, I have never forgotten it. Throughout the years I have often sought her advice in prayer. She has never failed me.

I could well apply the words of the *Memorare* to both our Blessed Mother and my own mother. "Never was it known that anyone who fled to your protection, implored your help, or sought your intercession was left unaided." Looking back on the years of my priestly ministry, I must admit that God has spoiled me. I have always been happy and peaceful, even when contrary winds gusted from time to time.

As I gazed longingly and lovingly at Mother's picture, I thanked her for her constant care and loving concern which I have experienced through the years. Like all good mothers, she always stood by me.

SIX

20-20 Vision

"Rabboni, . . . I want to see." (Mk 10:51)

I tried to visit Father Henry at least once a week. He was a dear old friend who had served the Lord long and well throughout many arduous years. When I visited him, I usually asked, "Well, Father, how are you today?" His answer was invariably the same. With a little chuckle he would respond: "To be honest about it, I am not seeing anyone today." That's right, Father Henry was blind.

Even though he had passed his eightieth birthday, he was still actively engaged in his own ministry. The path to his door was well-worn by people who sought his counsel. His life of intimate union with God in prayer enriched him with a wisdom and discernment that few have received. After Father Henry lost his eyesight, I put the Mass of the Blessed Virgin on tape so that he could review it occasionally, even though he had already memorized it. When he offered Mass, which he did daily, few people were aware that he was blind, so graceful were his actions and gestures.

A second friend, Dan, much younger than my priest friend, asked me if he could use my eyes. He too was blind. Dan spent long hours in prayer. He wanted to be in tune with the prayers of the church as presented in the Liturgy of the Hours. I was delighted to put these prayers on tape for him.

On one occasion Jesus said, "'If one blind man leads another, both will end in a pit'" (Mt 15:14). Jesus did not say anything about a blind man leading a person who is enjoying perfect vision. That is precisely what happened to me. Both of these friends, each in his own way, led me closer to the Lord.

In the first place, both Father Henry and Dan had a marvelous sense of humor. They were always cheerful and very much at peace. In fact, they regarded their handicap as a blessing in disguise.

Their attitude made me pause to reflect on my many blessings. I can see! I can behold the beauty of a landscape. I can look off to a distant horizon and then read from a printed page without any noticeable refocusing. I can enjoy the beauty of my family and friends. The list goes on.

Dan once wrote to me:

Through your lips, you have transmitted to me
that which your eyes perceived on the printed page.

It is worth more than gold to me,
for by your loving eyes and lips
I can see!

With blind Bartimaeus I pray, "'Rabboni, . . . I want to see'" (Mk 10:51). I want not merely to see with my eyes, but with my mind and heart I want to see and appreciate the multitudinous blessings of the Lord.

SEVEN

A Last Request

"O death, where is your victory?" (1 Cor 15:55)

Two very dear friends of mine, Don and Vivian, came to me with a rather unusual request. At first the request startled me, then I felt some anxiety. My hesitation was caused not by the nature of their request but by my feelings of inadequacy in fulfilling it. After brief reflection, however, I was overjoyed to say yes, I'd do what they asked, to the best of my ability.

Don, a model husband and father of five children, had just received a definitive diagnosis of terminal cancer. Before this sickness completely incapacitated him, the family wanted to make a weekend retreat together. They asked if I would give them a series of talks. In all my years in the priesthood and in my long involvement in the retreat ministry, this was the first time that I had ever been asked to give this special kind of retreat to a family who would soon lose their husband and father.

The whole weekend was a deeply moving experience for me and for all of them. There was a mixture of joy and peace, accompanied by a generous flow of tears.

Don summed it up in words similar to these: "We came together to share with one another, to pray together, to cry with one another, to seek comfort and consolation in each other, and also to smile and laugh together." At the closing Liturgy, surrounded by this family, I administered the sacrament of the anointing of the sick to Don.

Throughout his entire illness, Don never lost his smile nor his sense of humor. He was eager to encourage and assure others, not only the members of his own family but everyone who came to visit him. He often spoke about heaven and the meeting he expected to have with one of their daughters who had died a few years before.

In the closing weeks of his life on earth, Don initiated an apostolate of his own. During the retreat I had given him a book entitled *Living Here and Hereafter*, which is a series of scriptural reflections on eternal life. Don found much inspiration, comfort, and consolation in the words of this book.

Thereafter, when anyone visited him and tried to express their sympathy or found it difficult to understand God's plan in taking away such a young father, Don would bring out a copy of *Living Here and Hereafter* and offer it to them with a twofold request: first, that they promise to read the book; and second, that they pass it on to someone else. He managed to distribute some thirty copies before the Lord called him home.

The final days of Don's earthly sojourn were filled with great peace. His radiance reflected a life lived for the Lord, for his family, and for his fellowmen. His many friends gave testimony to their appreciation and their love for him by filling the church to overflowing on the day of his funeral. Don's life and his death gave me a richer appreciation of St. Paul's triumphant exclamation: " 'Death is swallowed up in victory.' 'O death, where is your victory? O death, where is your sting?'" (1 Cor 15:54-55).

EIGHT

The Name Is Kelly

Behold, sons are a gift from the LORD;
 the fruit of the womb is a reward. (Ps 127:3)

It was still very early in the morning when my phone jangled loud and clear. It was Tom announcing that Rita had just delivered their fourth baby—a girl—and they were going to call her Kelly. Yes, all had gone well, and mother and baby were doing fine. He suggested that I stop at the hospital to pay a visit to the women in his life.

I congratulated Tom on becoming a father for the fourth time, but this time it was different—this was their first girl. I promised that since this was my visiting day at the hospital, I would certainly drop into Room 407 to welcome Kelly to our world.

Later in the day I arrived in Rita's room to find her almost ecstatic with joy. She told me that when they brought the baby to her for the first time, she had the same contemplative experience that she had had at the birth of her three sons, only this time it was an even deeper, richer experience. She said that no dictionary contains words to describe how she felt. She had a sense of the divine presence in this new life which would last for an eternity. She concluded, "What a precious gift God gave me in the gift of motherhood!"

I rejoiced with Rita, congratulated her, and agreed that motherhood was really a share in God's creative power. She interrupted my good wishes to express her regret that in our confused culture many men and women do not appreciate the role of parenting. It is either downplayed or not mentioned at all. The feminist movement has deflected many women from their privileged vocation as wife and mother. She said rather ruefully, "It seems to be more important to become a lawyer or a business executive than to be a mother these days."

Rita had recently read of a study in which psychologists found that as more and more women abdicated their role in the home, their preschool children in day-care centers are showing increasing signs of neglect. Rita added that some of her own peers questioned the advisability of having so many children. In fact, one of the nurses on duty had intimated the same sentiment. "I wish I could share my joy with them," she concluded as the nurse brought in her newborn babe.

When I observed how tenderly Rita cradled the little one in her arms, I could not help but visualize Mary cuddling the baby Jesus in her arms in the cave in Bethlehem. Of course, I have to admit that I am slightly prejudiced, since Rita is my niece.

Part II

Performances

NINE

Steering Power

"Should anyone press you into service for one mile, go with him two miles." (Mt 5:41)

Most of us have had the experience of contending with rush-hour traffic. Some of us must deal with this situation daily. When office buildings and factories pour an endless flow of vehicles into our streets and freeways, bedlam can result. If an accident or road repair causes several lanes of traffic to be funneled into one or two lanes, the confusion mounts.

This is an opportune time to make a study of personalities. We find a whole gamut of reactions— some favorable, most not so edifying. Some drivers have learned to take it in stride. They seem almost oblivious to the inconvenience caused by the horde of vehicles hemming them in. Most drivers, however, become extremely impatient. There is usually a crescendo of horn blowing, from a little tooting to some prolonged, deafening blasts that jangle the nerves. Motors are revved, and cars jog back and forth in limited space, contributing even more to the general confusion.

It is amazing how personalities can change when people get behind a steering wheel. We may know people who are normally congenial, kind, considerate, and solicitous toward others, but who readily become angry and insulting when driving in traffic. They may crowd other cars simply to get a short distance ahead.

A sidewalk along a busy street gives one a privileged

observation deck to study the personalities of those in autos and other vehicles. On one occasion I was waiting in front of a large office building. A woman was double-parked because her car had stalled. She was having some difficulty in getting it started again; the motor simply would not respond in spite of her coaxing. The disgruntled driver in back of her opened his window to vocalize rather loudly his impatience and displeasure at being delayed. I am sure that this man would be very polite if he met this woman under other circumstances, but in this situation he ranted like a caged tiger.

Many people seem to experience a certain sense of power when a vehicle responds to a touch on the gas pedal. They often become belligerent when their supposed rights are threatened. On this occasion the woman kept her composure. She got out of her car, went back to the impatient, horn-blowing, vociferous driver, and said in a calm voice, "Sir, I seem to have difficulty in getting my car started. If you would be kind enough to try to start my car for me, I will stay here and blow your horn for you." I often wonder if Jesus foresaw this confusion and flaring of tempers when he advised us, "Should anyone press you into service for one mile, go with him two miles" (Mt 5:41).

TEN

Behind the Wheel

Live in accord with the spirit. (Gal 5:16)

I stopped at a traffic light on Beacon Boulevard on a beautiful summer afternoon. The instant the light hinted at turning green, the driver behind me started to toot his horn. In the meantime a woman headed in the opposite direction had her blinker light on, indicating her desire to make a left turn. As I proceeded through the intersection, she shouted that I should have permitted her to make the turn first. Had I no respect for a woman?

As I drove down the boulevard at the speed limit, the driver behind me kept gunning his motor. He finally shot around me, even though we were in a residential area. He shouted something at me as he sailed by. No, it is not repeatable.

I could see myself in both these drivers. I can become very impatient when traffic is heavy. I am annoyed at slow drivers. A stop light seems to be of longer duration when I am in a hurry. I think I am one of those gentle, gracious persons who become aggressive, selfish, and independent when driving a car.

Is it the sense of power that transforms us? Do we feel safe and protected in a car? In any case, it is disturbing to me how my brokenness, my self-centeredness, comes out when I am driving.

I am making a serious effort to reform. Jesus did not drive a car; hence he has not given me any specific directives. I am attempting to use every traffic sign and traffic turmoil to inspire within me a prayerful thought about God. It works sometimes.

When I drive up to a yield sign, I offer myself to the Lord once again, giving him everything I am doing at the time. I remind myself that I must yield to his plans and will for me. A stop sign triggers a reminder that I must pause throughout the day to recall the presence and power of the Lord in my life.

When my progress is encumbered by heavy traffic, especially during the commuting hours, I ask a blessing on the pedestrians or on those driving in the opposite direction. When the traffic speed seems very limiting, I recall that St. Paul told us to walk in the Spirit, not to run.

On one occasion a sister and I were caught in the Friday afternoon traffic on a Los Angeles freeway. We were moving bumper to bumper, with a whole series of delays in between. Sister suggested that we pray. Would you believe it, the moment we finished praying, the traffic thinned out and we were able to move more rapidly! Was it the power of intercession, or a natural "thinning out" place? I do not know. All I know is I became much calmer as we prayed.

Happy motoring!

ELEVEN

The Prowling Enemy

Your opponent the devil is prowling like a roaring lion.
(1 Pt 5:8)

While staying in a strange city, I was taking my early morning walk along a route that had been suggested to me. The road led through a zoo. As I was peacefully hiking along, I came upon a bridge, which rose several feet above the roadway. I walked up the little incline and started across. Then the morning stillness was shattered by the roar of a lion just below the bridge. I must have leaped high in the air, but I was too paralyzed by fear to run.

After I had recovered sufficiently, I discovered that I was on safe ground high above the enclosure of the lion. I looked down at this king of beasts, only to find him gazing up toward me. Apparently he was accustomed to having his breakfast about this time of the day. He must have mistaken me for the zoo attendant.

As we looked at each other, I tried to tell him that I had no food for him and he would have to wait. I continued my walk, still trembling in my running shoes. I am sure that my pace was faster now, as I wanted to put a little distance between me and the lion whose sleep I had interrupted. I cast a furtive glance over my shoulder, wanting to assure myself that the lion had not found a way out of his habitat.

After I had covered some distance, my pace became more relaxed. When I walk or jog I usually take time to meditate, often trying to recall some Scripture passage. The first thought that came to mind after I slowed down was from the psalmist's lyric account of creation:

> Young lions roar for the prey
> and seek their food from God. (Ps 104:21)

The roar that had almost sent me into orbit must have been the lion's prayer for food. Hopefully his keeper arrived soon afterward to satisfy his hunger.

As I walked along, I recalled St. Peter's powerful metaphor about our spiritual welfare: "Your opponent the devil is prowling like a roaring lion looking for someone to devour" (1 Pt 5:8). These words struck me forcefully after my encounter just a short time before.

The author of Proverbs says of the king of beasts, "The lion, mightiest of beasts, who retreats before nothing" (Prv 30:30). This aptly describes the devil's vicious prowling in search of a victim.

While my lion friend was safely enclosed in his confined area, the devil is by no means restricted. Yes, I may meet him when I'm out jogging as well as elsewhere.

TWELVE

Clowning Is an Art

"As often as you did it for one of my least brothers, you did it for me." (Mt 25:40)

Once when I was in San Francisco, I was walking in the vicinity of Fisherman's Wharf, which is frequented by thousands of tourists each year. Suddenly a clown appeared. He began to follow a pedestrian down the sidewalk, mimicking the gait and gestures of the person, to the amusement of bystanders.

After going some distance, the clown reversed his steps and followed another pedestrian back up the sidewalk. He then disappeared into the doorway from which he had emerged. The crowd found this performance hilarious, as did the people he was mimicking. They were good sports and joined in the fun.

The clown's antics were not only entertaining but also therapeutic. Most of the crowd was made up of sauntering visitors who were curiously observing whatever attracted their fancy. Other pedestrians had been scurrying along, intent on various destinations or preoccupied with some sort of business. The clown's unexpected spectacle brought a ray of sunshine to all who witnessed it. They saw themselves reflected in his antics.

On another occasion I saw clowns serve as real lifesavers. It was at a rodeo. If a rider was thrown and then threatened by a bucking horse or by a steer, several clowns would perform some diversionary stunts to draw the angry animal's attention away from the fallen rider.

While clowns may seem to have a slap happy disposition, we must remember that they are also human.

They experience the same traumas that all of us have from time to time. The story is told of a sad-eyed man who went to a doctor with the hope of finding some relief from his deep depression. After a lengthy and thorough examination, the doctor advised him to take a trip to the circus playing in town at the time, to laugh and enjoy the performance of Clyde the Clown. The patient groaned, "I am Clyde!"

Clowns deserve our respect and gratitude because they do not allow their own pain and problems to cause them to turn in on themselves. As they don their costume and swing into their performance, they totally forget about themselves. They focus instead on the enjoyment they can bring to others. Clowns remind us that it is possible to transcend our own sufferings, frustrations, disappointments, and problems. They show us how important it is to develop a genuine sense of humor and to reach out in loving concern for others.

Clowns come under the blessing of Jesus: "'I assure you, as often as you did it for one of my least brothers, you did it for me'" (Mt 25:40).

THIRTEEN

Clowning for Christ

"That . . . your joy may be complete." (Jn 15:11)

I knew a gracious and dignified president of a large bank who several times a year donned his clown costume and went off to some institution or gathering to entertain crippled or hurting people. When I asked him about his avocation, he responded very humbly, "A clown can bring some joy and happiness into the lives of lonely and hurting people that no other type of entertainment can achieve. If I can cheer up these poor people a little and make their day a little brighter, I enjoy great satisfaction and fulfillment in my own life."

We might think of clowns as slap happy people who make fools of themselves just to entertain others. Yet clowns are entertaining because of the nature of their performance. They are students of human nature. For the most part they imitate the peculiar mannerisms of the people they entertain. They mimic our human idiosyncrasies and incongruities.

If we feel discouraged or depressed, clowns can raise our spirits. As they imitate our unique personal traits in walking, talking, and gesturing, they enable us to laugh at ourselves. We learn not to take ourselves or the world in which we live too seriously. These antics are really therapeutic.

Centuries ago clowns were greatly respected for their art. They were thought to possess the spirit of God in a special way, and thus were able to bring relief and joy to others.

Would it sound blasphemous to say that part of Jesus' ministry was similar to the role of a clown? Jesus often pointed out the ridiculous aberrations of our conduct and the attitudes that lead only to misery and unhappiness. Jesus reached out to the hurting people who flocked to him. What peace and joy he brought them! He revealed the good news to bring happiness and joy into our lives. Jesus' statement is brief but apt:

"All this I tell you
that my joy may be yours
and your joy may be complete." (Jn 15:11)

We too are to play the role of a clown at times. Jesus wants us to develop the capacity to reach out in loving concern, especially to those who are hurting. In the eyes of the world we may seem foolish in doing so. As St. Paul could say, "We have become a spectacle to the universe, to angels and men alike. We are fools on Christ's account" (1 Cor 4:9-10).

Part III

Ponderings

FOURTEEN

Did You Get the Message?

Listen, that you may have life. (Is 55:3)

A man once registered for a university course in telepathy. He paid his tuition fee, but after many weeks he had heard nothing from the university. When he called to check on the reason why he had not heard from them, he was told that they were sending him messages for the past few weeks. When he maintained that he had not heard any messages, they informed him that he had flunked the course.

We may find ourselves in a similar predicament. The Lord is sending us messages constantly. We may not be receiving them because of being absorbed in our own affairs.

In order to be aware of what the Lord is trying to convey to us, we must maintain an attitude of attentive receptivity. In brief, we must listen. Listening does not merely mean using our sense of hearing; it involves being wholly attuned to the Lord. It means being available to God.

Life presents a constant bombardment of noise and confusion. The telephone, the television, and the radio invade our privacy. To preserve our equilibrium, we have learned to turn off much of this noise. As a result we hear very much but we seldom listen.

Listening is an art. It means putting ourselves as much as we can in the position of the person speaking to us, trying to experience what he or she is feeling.

Listening is vital to good communication and

33

essential in establishing personal relationships. The axiom is trite but true: We cannot love a person we do not know, and we cannot really know a person unless we have listened to that person. There is a difference between knowing about a person and knowing a person. Only by listening can we know someone as a person—his likes and dislikes, his personality and character.

A person reveals much about himself or herself by conversation, by attitudes, and by actions. Only when we are familiar with these can we say that we know that person. This falsifies the notion of love at first sight, for we must first know a person before we can really love that person.

I fear that there are many people who go through life without really knowing God. We may know much about him theologically, but we also need to know him as a person. In order to know God as a person, we must listen to what he tells us about himself.

The Lord bids us come to him that we may get to know him. This is his invitation:

Come to me heedfully,
    listen, that you may have life. (Is 55:3)

The psalmist too begs us not to turn away, but to listen with our whole being:

Oh, that today your would hear his voice:
    "Harden not your hearts." (Ps 95:7-8)

Jesus came into the world to make the Father better known. In turn the Father says quite imperatively to us, "'This is my Son, my Chosen One. Listen to him'" (Lk 9:35).

FIFTEEN
Letters from Heaven

My word . . . shall not return to me void. (Is 55:11)

Some time ago I was visiting my family. The summer weather was so pleasant that we spent much time on the front porch. From this vantage point I could survey the street leading to the family home. Day after day I was impressed by the mail carrier.

He was a happy, joy-filled person. He knew everyone. If someone was out-of-doors, he would greet them in a very personal way, inquiring about the family or commenting on the beauty of the flowers or the welcoming shade of a tree in the front yard. He was more than a person who delivers mail each day; he was a friend of everyone along the street.

As I noticed this man's cheerful disposition and his radiant personality, I thought too about the letters he was delivering. We all welcome mail delivery time. We eagerly sort through the mail to discover whether or not we have received a personal letter from a dear one. Bills and second-class mail receive our attention only later.

Personal letters are important. They bring us good news and update us on happenings among our family and friends. As we read a letter, the writer becomes very present to us. We can almost hear his or her voice. A letter ranks next in line to a personal visit.

A letter speaks another important message, one that we hear not with our external sense of hearing but deep down inside us. The letter tells us that the sender cares enough to take the time and effort to write to us and to communicate with us.

There is a very special category of mail: love letters. How eagerly a person awaits them! How avidly the content is devoured! They are read many times over and then treasured, often tied with a blue ribbon and put into safekeeping for years to come.

Whether our courting days have come and gone—or perhaps they never were for whatever reason—you and I still receive countless love letters. I'm speaking of God's letters to us as found in Scripture. His letters are to be read, reread, reflected upon, contemplated, and totally absorbed. In order that they may become a part of us, we must read them slowly and consistently, permitting every word to penetrate our being and ultimately to find a home in our heart.

A letter from a loved one makes that person very present to us. Scripture does even more, since Jesus himself is present in his word. Furthermore, there is a transforming power in God's love letters to us. The Lord himself said:

> Just as from the heavens
>   the rain and snow come down
> And do not return there
>   till they have watered the earth,
>   making it fertile and fruitful, . . .
> So shall my word be
>   that goes forth from my mouth;
> It shall not return to me void,
>   but shall do my will,
>   achieving the end for which I sent it. (Is 55:10-11)

St. Paul, in his marvelous collection of letters, speaks very explicitly about God's "love letters" to us: "All Scripture is inspired of God and is useful for teaching—for reproof, correction, and training in holiness so that the man of God may be fully competent and equipped for every good work" (2 Tm 3:16-17).

Even though the postal rates may soar sky-high, let us keep on writing. It is a mission of love. Let us also read the love letters we all have on hand—God's own words to us in Scripture.

SIXTEEN

Words, Words

He who restrains his lips does well. (Prv 10:19)

I knew an elderly priest, long since gone to his eternal reward, who had a wealth of unusual and humorous expressions which he used generously in his conversation. He seemed adept at responding with some sort of witticism on every occasion. When I encouraged him to make a thesaurus of these witty remarks, he informed me that humor depends upon spontaneity, and such a collection would lack luster if taken out of context. He was right, but we are poorer because of it.

On one occasion someone detained this priest for a long period of time with much idle talk. He later described the person as a *sine fine dicentes* person. The preface of the old Latin Mass always ended with these words, which mean "saying without end."

Sometimes words are devoid of meaning. This is expressed in Shakespeare's play *Hamlet*. When Polonius was curious about what Hamlet was reading, Hamlet covered up his pretense by responding, "Words, words, words."

One day as I was passing a construction site, I

overheard a workman say to his partner, "I'm telling you for the last time." His fellow worker responded, "Sure, you're telling me, but you ain't said nothing yet."

People often try to shield their insecurity with a wall of words. Others strive to gain acceptance by using volumes of "impressive" words. Still others try to hide their real feelings and intent behind words. Don't we all use an abundance of words when we are trying to excuse ourselves from a duty that is expected of us?

As we listen to someone speak, we must strive to penetrate the flow of words and comprehend what the person is really saying. Consider the child who comes to his mother with a supposedly injured finger and asks for a bandaid. What the child is really saying is "Mother, I want your attention. I want your loving care and concern." Haven't we played a similar game at times?

An infant begins its babbling with "da da" or some similar syllables. You might consider these utterances meaningless syllables, but never tell a mother that. True, there are words that only a mother can understand and interpret.

On the other hand, the author of the Book of Proverbs warns us about the multiplicity of words:

Where words are many, sin is not wanting;
    but he who restrains his lips does well. (Prv 10:19)

James, the first bishop of Jerusalem, confirms this: "If a person is without fault in speech he is a man in the fullest sense, because he can control his entire body" (Jas 3:2).

It behooves me to terminate these thoughts immediately; otherwise I might be labeled a *sine fine dicentes* person.

SEVENTEEN
More about Words

"I will welcome you and be a father to you." (2 Cor 6:18)

Joan and I have many lively discussions. She never misses an occasion to remind me that the language of the Bible is sexist. She places all the blame on our modern translators. I hasten to remind her that she should not sit in judgment on the translators. For centuries they have been trying to convey in our modern languages the exact meaning of the original codices, and they have found it very difficult.

We must admit that English is rather recent as far as languages go. Give us a few hundred years, and we will have a richer, more descriptive language.

Since Joan is an English teacher and has worked with lexicographers, I asked her what she thought was the precise function of words. This question brought an immediate and professional response.

As I recall her answer, the first function of words is to convey information. Words are the most common and efficient way to let someone know something.

Second, words tell us something about the speaker. When we speak we reveal something about ourselves— our feelings and attitudes, our likes and dislikes.

Third, when we speak or write, we involve another person in a relationship. We might initiate a new relationship, or we might deepen an existing one. On the other hand, words can create an unfavorable or even a hostile reaction.

I found Joan's insights helpful, and I proceeded to apply them to the words of the Bible. God has revealed his truths to us through the words of Scripture. It is a rich storehouse of information. Likewise God reveals very much about himself by his words. We discover that he is a loving, caring, forgiving God. Jesus also tells us much about himself through his speech.

As we listen to God's words, we begin to establish a relationship with him. When we hear him say, "You are precious to me and I love you," we instinctively want to respond to him in love. When Jesus says, "There is no greater love than this: to lay down one's life for one's friends," our hearts swell with gratitude.

At this point in our discussion, Joan accused me of deliberately diverting the conversation from her original objection to the language in the Bible. I assured her that the Lord is not responsible for the expressions as translated, for he says:

> "'I will welcome you and be a father to you
> and you will be my sons and daughters,'
> says the Lord Almighty." (2 Cor 6:18)

EIGHTEEN

The First and Last Word

And the Word was God. (Jn 1:1)

Some time ago my younger brother was suffering from cancer of the throat. After surgery he was unable to speak, nor was he able to master his portable voice box. It was difficult to communicate with him. We could speak to him, but his response was usually a gesture or a smile stretching from ear to ear. It was then that I began to realize how important words are as vehicles of our thoughts and our feelings. The Lord has blessed us in giving us the ability to communicate with one another through words.

Any time I am in a foreign land, I get very frustrated

in trying to convey a message to someone whose language I cannot speak. I recall one occasion when a venerable, gray-haired rabbi conducted me on a tour through the synagogue in Nazareth. I was extremely curious about the Jewish method of prayer and worship. I had an abundance of questions, but I was not sufficiently fluent in Hebrew to go beyond some general greetings. Again the function of words was impressed upon me.

I asked myself, what would our world be like without words? It is difficult to imagine. Without words we would lack a lot of information. Without words we could have a melody but no lyrics. Without words we would have nothing to read for our instruction or enjoyment. Without words our telephones would be useless. Without words we would have no greeting cards at Christmas time or on birthdays and anniversaries. There would be no correspondence from home.

If words did not exist, we would know very little about God. Through the words of the prophets and sages of the Old Testament, we know God as our creating, caring Father who provides for us at every moment of the day.

Our world of words begins with God as the Word. When God wanted his Word to be known, loved, and lived in a brand new way, he sent him into the world:

In the beginning was the Word;
    the Word was in God's presence;
    and the Word was God. . . .
    The Word became flesh
    and made his dwelling among us. (Jn 1:1, 14)

Jesus often referred to his word as the norm and guideline for our daily living. "Blest are they who hear the word of God and keep it" (Lk 11:28).

What an extravagant promise Jesus made when he said:

> "Anyone who loves me
> will be true to my word,
> and my Father will love him;
> we will come to him
> and make our dwelling place with him." (Jn 14:23)

Part IV

Parables

NINETEEN

Beneath the Dome of the Sky

All you birds of the air, bless the Lord. (Dn 3:80)

The water bubbled into the first pan of the birdbath, then gently overflowed into the two lower pans. I sat very quietly, watching the birds arrive in great numbers to quench their thirst and to enjoy some splashing in the refreshing water. The scene before me would have been a bird-watcher's delight.

I began to notice the elegant plumage of the different species of birds. Each had its own distinct markings. Each feather had its own unique design, from the robin to the magpie, to the goldfinch, down to the lowly sparrow.

What works of art! Each bird reflected the creative genius of our glorious God. How simply the inspired writer speaks of God's ongoing creative power: "God said.... 'On the earth let the birds fly beneath the dome of the sky.'. . . God created. . . . all kinds of winged birds. . . God blessed them saying . . . 'Let the birds multiply on the earth'" (Gn 1:20-22).

God empowered every species with its own special ability to adapt to its environment and way of life. The quail runs with astounding speed, the eagle soars on the wind, and most birds escape danger because of their alertness and their ability to fly at great speeds.

The Father's love for the birds and even more so for us is a caring, concerned love. How generously he provides for all his creation. Jesus taught us a valuable lesson when he used the birds as an example. He said,

"'Look at the birds in the sky. They do not sow or reap, they gather nothing into barns; yet your heavenly Father feeds them.'" Then he added his punch line: "'Are not you more important than they?'" (Mt 6:26).

Our gracious Father provides for us in thousands of different ways. He not only provides for our sustenance, but he created the birds for our pleasure and enjoyment. Have we not often been thrilled to hear the birds filling the early morning air with their melodious song? Have we not wondered how those tiny throats can send out their joyous notes to such great distances? Have we not gazed in wonder at the plumage of a peacock strutting before us or at the beauty of a pet parakeet? We could go on about hundreds more species.

Tertullian visualized the birds in prayer. He wrote: "The birds too rise and lift themselves up to heaven; they open out their wings, instead of hands, in the form of a cross, and give voice to what seems to be a prayer" (II LH 250).

The inspired writer of the Book of Daniel calls upon all creation, including birds, to praise and glorify the God of all creation:

All you birds of the air, bless the Lord;
    praise and exalt him above all forever. (Dn 3:80)

Let us too praise God for and with the birds!

TWENTY

Pass the Salt, Please

"You are the salt of the earth." (Mt 5:13)

How casually during the course of a meal we ask someone to pass the salt or pick it up ourselves to sprinkle a little on our food. Salt is one of the many precious gifts of God that we are apt to take for granted. It satisfies special needs in our lives.

In ancient times people valued salt very highly. The Romans maintained that *nil utilius sole et sale*, "there is nothing more useful than the sun and salt."

Salt is richly symbolic. Its glistening whiteness is probably the reason it was chosen as the symbol of purity. In order to purify their sacrifices, the pagans of old used to offer salt to their gods. Salt was also used in Jewish sacrifices.

Salt has always been highly regarded as a preservative. The ancient Greek writer Plutarch maintained that it added a new soul and a new life to matter. Even with our modern techniques of refrigeration, salt is still used as a preservative.

Perhaps we appreciate salt most as a condiment. Just a little pinch of it can flavor a whole meal. A little dash of it can make the food on our plate much more palatable. In fact, some of us have a tendency to use too much salt, which can cause some medical problems.

Jesus paid us a great compliment when he said to us, his followers, "'You are the salt of the earth'" (Mt 5:13). After two thousand years, we often use the same expression when we wish to express our appreciation to another: "You are the salt of the earth."

Jesus' compliment is also a challenge for us. If we are the salt of the earth, we must represent everything that salt symbolizes.

As Christians we must permit the glistening whiteness of our lives to shine forth. We must keep ourselves unstained by the world in which we live. Jesus expresses this challenge in another way: "'Your light must shine before men so that they may see goodness in your acts and give praise to your heavenly Father'" (Mt 5:26).

Like salt, we too must have a purifying influence on

others. We can exercise this power in many different ways. When there are hurts and misunderstandings, we may be called upon to bring peace. When advocating a certain way of life is not the most popular position, we must dare to be different.

A little salt goes a long way. We may be only a little pinch of salt in our environment, but our influence to flavor is indeed powerful. Our sense of humor, the peace and joy that radiate from us, can touch the lives of many people. Our loving concern for others can be a great witness to the little world in which we move.

The next time someone asks you to pass the salt, you might recall that Jesus said, "You are the salt of the earth," and, "Your light must shine before men so that they may see goodness in your acts and give praise to your heavenly Father."

TWENTY-ONE

Thumbing Our Way

"No follower of mine shall ever walk in darkness."

(Jn 8:12)

The other day I sprained my thumb slightly. The little inconvenience it caused me started a whole train of reflections about my thumb. With a sprained thumb it was hard for me to pick up a tiny pin, tie my shoes, write a note, or even eat a meal in my normal fashion.

I was discovering how useful my thumb really is. How wisely God equipped us with thumbs! I do not recall ever thanking God specifically for my thumb until I injured mine and could not use it. How readily we take God's gifts for granted.

My thumbprint establishes my unique identity;

there is no other exactly like it. I am a unique, unrepeatable miracle of God's creative love. Likewise, there are no two leaves exactly alike, no two snow-flakes, no two grains of sand.

Our thumbs can say a lot. When we are bored, we twiddle our thumbs. In the days of the Roman gladiators, "thumbs down" meant death, and "thumbs up" was a vote for freedom. Clumsy people are said to be "all thumbs." Some people stick out "like sore thumbs."

In Old Testament times, warriors defeated in battle had their thumbs and big toes cut off. This mutilation incapacitated them as fighters. There is such an account in the Book of Judges: "Adonibezek fled. They set out in pursuit, and when they caught him, cut off his thumbs and his big toes. At this Adonibezek said, 'Seventy kings, with their thumbs and big toes cut off, used to pick up scraps under my table. As I have done, so has God repaid me'" (Jgs 1:6-7).

When a person hitchhikes, we say that he is "thumbing his way." Figuratively speaking, we are all hitchhikers thumbing our way through life. Fortu-nately Jesus is standing by, willing to travel with us. How badly we need him at times, when our journey through life becomes complicated. We do not have a clear road map to guide us every step of the way.

We need the companionship and encouragement of Jesus as we climb the hills or descend into the valleys that we encounter on our journey. Jesus reassures us: "Know that I am with you always, until the end of the world" (Mt 28:20).

We need the Lord's guidance when we come to the many unmarked crossroads on the roadway of life. How easily we can lose our way when the darkness and dreariness of life envelop us! Again Jesus comes to our rescue as we thumb our way. He tells us:

> "I am the light of the world.
> No follower of mine shall ever walk in darkness;
> no, he shall possess the light of life." (Jn 8:12)

Jesus joins us along our journey just as he accompanied the disciples on the road to Emmaus. We need to pause to recall his promises that he would be with us always and that he would never leave us. Thumbing our way through life with Jesus will make our journey peaceful, joyous, and delightful.

We need to remember that our thumbs and all that we are and all that we have are God's gifts to us. How we use these gifts will determine the degree of our own happiness. When we use the gifts with which God endowed us in the manner that God intended, then we are glorifying him. Being grateful for our thumbs is one way of expressing our gratitude to our all-good God.

TWENTY-TWO

One Loaf

We . . . are one body, for we all partake of the one loaf.
(1 Cor 10:17)

As I munched on a mammoth sandwich which I had assembled, I started thinking about the two huge slices of bread that encased the lettuce, bacon, and tomato of my creation. I don't know if it was because of the satisfying taste of what I was eating or just the mood I was in, but my mind took off on a flight of reflection.

I asked myself some unanswerable questions: How

many grains of wheat did it require to make the flour for this loaf of bread? How many people were involved in planting, nurturing, and harvesting the wheat? How many were needed to transport, mill, and bake this loaf of bread? As I tried to visualize all the people who might have been involved, my mind began to reel.

Continuing to munch, I thought about how each grain of wheat had to be ground and milled into fine flour for baking. Like the grain of wheat, we too have been created to perform some special role in God's divine plan. Jesus told us that in order to become his followers we had to die to ourselves. He compared us to grains of wheat:

"I solemnly assure you,
unless the grain of wheat falls to the earth and dies,
it remains just a grain of wheat.
But if it dies, it produces much fruit. . . .
The man who hates his life in this world
preserves it to life eternal." (Jn 12:24-25)

The mystery of Jesus' own sacrifice is perpetuated in the Eucharist. Jesus used bread because it is symbolic of what his eucharistic presence should mean in our lives. It gives us life and love. It has a unifying power, calling us to form Christian community. St. Paul's metaphor is right to the point: "And is not the bread we break a sharing in the body of Christ? Because the loaf of bread is one, we, many though we are, are one body, for we all partake of the one loaf" (1 Cor 10:16-17).

The Eucharist can heal us of our self-centeredness and enable us to reach out in loving concern to others. It is this love that welds us together in Christian community.

Bread has rightly been called the staff of life. The eucharistic bread is certainly the staff of our spiritual growth and maturation. All this springs from a tiny grain of wheat.

By this time all that remained of my sandwich was a few scattered crumbs. Instead of brushing them away, I reverently gathered them up and ate them appreciatively.

TWENTY-THREE

Rings

A man's goodness God cherishes like a signet ring.
(Sir 17:17)

My beautiful young niece literally danced around the room from one person to another. She was proudly displaying for our inspection and admiration the diamond engagement ring she had just received. Amid the congratulations and good wishes there was genuine rejoicing, for it seemed to all of us that her forthcoming marriage was certainly one of those arranged in heaven. This young couple seemed ideally suited to one another.

My niece was radiant, and her ring was beautiful. Its faceted diamond sparkled in every direction. On my way home I started to think more about the significance of rings.

A ring is a sacred symbol. It speaks of love, dedication, commitment. Its circular band symbolizes a permanent commitment. As a constant companion to the wearer, it is a reminder of the agreement between two people. It is also a reminder that every undertaking throughout the day is a part of that total commitment.

Rings are usually worn by vowed persons. Husband and wife are vowed to each other under God. Priests, religious, and some lay people are vowed to God in the service of others. In each of these cases a ring bears witness to the world of the commitment these people have made.

My mother was called to her eternal reward before I was ordained a priest. Her wedding band, now mounted immediately under the cup of my chalice, is a daily reminder of her dedication and commitment to God and to her family. The sight of that ring supports me in times of vexation and discouragement. Not only does it remind me of her life of sacrifice for me and for the rest of the family, but it also reminds me that she is continuing her intercession for us from her place in heaven.

I am delighted when a mother displays her "mother's ring," with the birthstones of her children mounted in it. Such a ring bespeaks a life of loving dedication.

When the prodigal son returned home, he asked only to be readmitted to his father's house as a servant. But the father ordered that a ring be put on his finger. The ring symbolized a full and complete reinstatement into the family, with all the rights and authority that family membership carried with it.

In former days a signet ring was used to impress a wax seal to authenticate letters and documents sent out by an official. If a person gave a signet ring to another, he was really giving him the power of attorney. The person receiving the signet ring was able to act and speak in the name of the one who had given him the ring. The signet rings of bishops and the pope originated at this time.

Going back even further in time, when Pharaoh put Joseph in charge of the whole land of Egypt, he took off his signet ring and put it on Joseph's finger. Pharaoh said, "'You shall be in charge of my palace, and all my people shall dart at your command'" (Gn 41:40).

Trying to express in words how pleased God is with men's good works, Sirach says:

A man's goodness God cherishes like a signet ring,
a man's virtue, like the apple of his eye. (Sir 17:17)

TWENTY-FOUR

Gifts from the Table

"I have greatly desired to eat this Passover with you."
(Lk 22:15)

Have you ever observed the many shapes, sizes, and styles of tables or the multiplicity of uses that tables serve? There are oval tables in meeting rooms, picnic tables in parks, display tables in stores. Every office boasts tables for typewriters, computers, and lamps, as well as tabletops that serve as work areas. In our homes we find dining and kitchen tables, end tables, laundry tables, work tables, and so on. The table is certainly the workhorse among furniture.

In my growing-up years our kitchen table was the focal point of all our family activities. Our spacious kitchen was a natural place for the family to gather. The large table there was not the most comfortable place to sit and visit, but it became the hub of family activity. There we could catch up on the day's happenings. There we found a note if someone called while we were out. There our folded laundry awaited our taking it to our rooms. If we wanted to leave some article, such as a key, for another member of the family, it was often left on the kitchen table. If we arrived home some time before a regular meal, we always found some goodies awaiting us.

Each week we had a family meeting around the kitchen table. Our plans, programs, and projects were discussed and formulated.

Some of the happiest memories of my childhood are of the meals we shared around our kitchen table. It made little difference whether the food was festive or simple; the highlight was the joy we found in each other and in what each person had experienced that day. My father was a master at granting each person equal time to talk. He often reminded us that the family that eats together stays together.

Our kitchen table also served as a sort of family altar. During the course of a meal my father would lead us in a time of prayer, which included thanking God for some favor of the day or praying for a special intention—perhaps a brother or sister was having an exam or facing a difficult task. At times, especially during Lent, we prayed the rosary around the kitchen table.

We often received some unsolicited catechetical instruction while seated around the kitchen table. I remember an occasion when one of us complained about the lengthy time we took for a meal and about the discomfort of sitting on hard chairs. My father responded with quite a lecture about the table at which Jesus reclined at the Last Supper and the lengthy time he took to reassure the apostles. He went on to explain that Jesus said the first Mass at the dining room table in the upper room. Even the altars in our churches are built like tables, he explained, because Jesus wants to share a meal with us.

These lessons in my early life were so thorough that they still bear fruit today. When I see food in abundance on a table, it brings to mind the extravagant goodness of our provident Father. I also learned that mealtime is a splendid occasion to enjoy the gifts that we are to one another.

In the spiritual realm the altar table is the fountain of the Lord's divine life and love, which nurture and nourish us, enabling us to meet the demands of each day. As we assemble around the altar at Mass, we can almost hear the Lord saying again, "'I have greatly desired to eat this Passover with you,'" which is followed by, "'Do this as a remembrance of me'" (Lk 22:15, 19).

Part V

Prayer

TWENTY-FIVE

When Are We Praying?

Never cease praying. (1 Thes 5:17)

Charlie, a dear friend of mine, is elderly and homebound. I try to visit him regularly. When I inquired about his health on my last visit, he quietly and uncomplainingly told me that he felt he was slipping a great deal. As a criterion he said, "I can't even pray anymore. All I can do now is just talk to God."

It was a joy for me to assure him that he was praying and that perhaps his prayer was far more pleasing to God than if he were able to recite many long formulae of prayer. I explained to him that prayer is our relationship to our loving Father. We can express that relationship in countless ways.

Margaret lives in the same building and is now approaching her eighty-fifth birthday. When I told her that Charlie and I had talked about prayer, she said that her prayer too is different from what it used to be. She said that when she thinks of God's immense goodness to her throughout her long years, she just breathes a deep sigh and asks Jesus to accept it as a thank you and a love offering. When she thinks of all the bad things she did in her life, she simply strikes her breast. I must add that this is quite an effort for Margaret, since she is very arthritic and every movement is painful.

Surely both Margaret and Charlie have entered into a prayerful union with the Lord. Merely turning our gaze and attention to the Lord is prayer. I have assured both of them that they are the great prayer power in the church and that we were counting upon their intercessions.

59

St. Paul gives us some direct admonitions about prayer: "Pray perseveringly, be attentive to prayer, and pray in a spirit of thanksgiving" (Col 4:2). And: "Never cease praying, render constant thanks" (1 Thes 5:17-18).

This is a tall order, for certainly we cannot spend all our waking hours in prayer. Prayer is attitudinal and relational. It is a matter of committing ourselves totally to the Lord in all that we do, say, and are.

I am reminded of a retired bishop, a saintly and humble person. Alzheimer's disease was beginning to take its toll, but he did have some lucid moments. When I made some remark about what was happening to him, his immediate response was, "I gave God my whole life to do with as he wills. If he wants my mind as well, I gladly and freely offer it to him." That is praying unceasingly.

I have my own way of reminding myself of the presence of the Trinity within me. I usually enjoy an early morning cup of coffee before our household stirs. As I sip in peaceful quiet and solitude and feel the coffee's warmth in my mouth and throat, I think of the Trinity filling me with divine love. Some may question this as a prayer, but it does help me think of the presence and power of the Lord dwelling within me. I hope the Lord doesn't mind this prayer posture.

TWENTY-SIX

Kneel to Stand Tall

"Here I stand, knocking at the door." (Rv 3:20)

After the hubbub of the Christmas festivities settles down, I enjoy taking some time to study the Christmas cards I received. Pondering these cards thoughtfully and reflectively has become a prayerful experience for me.

The last time I did so, I made a new discovery. A large percentage of the cards I received depicted Mary kneeling at the manger of her divine Son in silent reverence, while Joseph, in a standing position, looked on in quiet admiration. It suddenly struck me that these two positions are both splendid prayer postures.

Mary's kneeling position touched me very deeply. As she gazed in awe at her Son, her smiling eyes radiated the love and joy pouring out of her heart. Mary is not merely a young mother lovingly beholding her firstborn son, but she is kneeling in recognition of who her Son is. Her silent adoration is indicative of her total submission to the privileged role for which she was chosen. This was the first time that Mary's kneeling posture impressed me so forcefully.

Kneeling is a petitioning posture. We can picture a young man kneeling before a young woman as he asks for her hand in marriage. Kneeling is almost always associated with prayer. It acknowledges God as Creator, Redeemer, and providing Father. It is also a sign of humility. When we kneel, we sacrifice one-third of our height. We want to stand tall before our friends and associates. In prayer we kneel before God so that we can stand tall before men.

Standing is also a proper prayer posture. It is a stance of reverence and respect. It manifests a willingness to be of service. Standing when a special person enters a room is a sign of respect. In the military an enlisted person or even an officer stands at attention when a superior officer is present. A guard stands prepared to protect whatever is entrusted to his custody. I have often wondered if the great prophet Isaiah was standing when he responded to the Lord,

"Here I am, . . . send me" (Is 6:8).

Whatever our prayer posture, Jesus is at our beck and call when we go to him. Did he not assure us, "'Here I stand, knocking at the door. If anyone hears me calling and opens the door, I will enter his house and have supper with him, and he with me'" (Rv 3:20)?

We need to remember that Jesus is a gentleman. He does not force himself on us but waits for our invitation. We must also note that the latch is on the inside of the door.

TWENTY-SEVEN

Raising Hands

To you I stretch out my hands. (Ps 88:10)

As I gazed at a perfectly shaped tree, its branches swaying gracefully in the gentle breeze, I was reminded of that verse from Joyce Kilmer's poem entitled "Trees":

"A tree that looks at God all day
and lifts her leafy arms to pray . . ."

The poet touches upon a very meaningful gesture of prayer. For a long time lifting one's hands in prayer was a regular custom, but then it faded into oblivion. Now this prayer posture is becoming common once again.

Raising our arms in prayer is an eloquent way of expressing some dispositions that are essential to sincere prayer. In the first place, lifting our hands with our palms open and upward is a way of expressing our total offering of self to the Lord. The one offering that the Lord desires is that of ourselves, with all that we are and all that we do. Making such an oblation to the

Lord enables him to mold and transform us into the kind of person he wants us to be.

Second, hands raised in prayer indicate our willingness to respond to whatever the Lord might ask of us. It is our way of asking the Lord for the grace and help we need to be open and receptive to whatever he wills for us. It is a gesture of acceptance as well as one of giving, leading us into a disposition for humble prayer.

Raising our hands in prayer is also a way of breaking down many of our inhibitions. It opens us to begin expressing ourselves honestly and sincerely.

My good friend Gordon told me that he was very disturbed by people's raising their hands in prayer. He thought it was too emotional and theatrical. In explaining to him the significance of this prayer posture, I pointed out that the priest at Mass often extends his hands in prayer in the same fashion. This is especially apparent at the introductory dialogue at the Preface. The priest says, "Lift up your hearts," and we respond, "We lift them up to the Lord."

I also reminded Gordon that the Psalter is the only book of divinely inspired prayers that we possess. The psalms frequently exhort us to lift our hands in prayer:

> Let my prayer come like incense before you;
> the lifting up of my hands, like the evening sacrifice. (Ps 141:2)
> I stretch out my hands to you;
> my soul thirsts for you like parched land.
> (Ps 143:6)
> Hear the sound of my pleading, when I cry to you,
> lifting up my hands toward your holy shrine.
> (Ps 28:2)
> Daily I call upon you, O LORD;
> to you I stretch out my hands. (Ps 88:10)

St. Paul adds his own admonition: "It is my wish, then, that in every place the men shall offer prayers with blameless hands held aloft, and be free from anger and dissension" (1 Tim 2:8).

These are only a few of the mentions in Scripture about this prayer posture. As I write these words, I find myself wanting to raise my hands in prayer. But my old typewriter needs my hands to translate my thoughts onto paper.

TWENTY-EIGHT

Dial Direct

"If anyone hears me calling . . . I will enter his house.'"
(Rv 3:20)

Fred and I were having a serious discussion in his office. His secretary was away at the time, and Fred had to answer the telephone himself. Several times in the course of our conversation we were interrupted by incoming calls. I was impressed by Fred's manner in answering the phone. He gave his undivided attention to the caller. He was courteous but always to the point, not wasting any time on idle chatter.

I was also amazed at Fred's ability to continue our conversation at the exact point where we were interrupted. I complimented him on this ability to maintain his train of thought.

Fred explained that he was able to do so because he made several long distance calls each day. I must have looked puzzled. He went on to explain that they were not the usual type of long distance calls. Rather, the phone was a reminder to him to get in touch with our loving Father in heaven several times throughout the day. These "calls" gave him inspiration, insight, and patience for the day.

He also told me that there were two other great advantages in calling on the Father. There is no charge. The Lord does not even have an 800 number. Furthermore, "You will never get a busy signal," he assured me.

I reminded Fred that the Lord is with us always and everywhere and that a long distance call to the transcendent God was not necessary. His answer was right on. He said, "The Lord does not need the phone to communicate with me, but I need it. The phone has become a symbol, a reminder for me that I must get in touch with the Lord periodically throughout the day; otherwise I become ruffled rather easily. This phone on my desk helps me to remember that I must stop occasionally and communicate with the Lord."

I was impressed by Fred's technique. I decided that I should discover and develop some such custom. I often get annoyed when the phone invades the privacy of a visit with a friend, or interrupts some engrossing work, or delays me when I am rushing to an appointment. I fear that I do not always accept these interruptions graciously.

During his time on earth Jesus did not have the convenience of a telephone, but he did remind us that he is always available and calling: "'Here I stand, knocking at the door. If anyone hears me calling and opens the door, I will enter his house and have supper with him, and he with me'" (Rv 3:20).

TWENTY-NINE

My Prayer Shelf

I love you, O LORD, my strength,
  O LORD, my rock, my fortress, my deliverer. (Ps 18:2)

This morning I received a letter from a young couple who are very dear to me. They informed me that their first baby had just been born and that mother and baby were doing fine. They also included a picture of the proud father gazing lovingly on mother and child. The annoucement said, "The father is recovering quite well."

After rereading the announcement, I placed it on my prayer shelf. I thanked the good Lord for all his creative and providential love, especially for this young couple. I whispered a little prayer for Gerry and Louise, asking God to bless them and guide them in rearing their offspring through the maze of daily living until she reaches her final home in heaven.

My prayer shelf is a very sacred place in my home, almost like a miniature altar. It displays quite an assortment of objects from time to time. These serve as reminders of the presence and power of God operating at every moment in my life.

In front of my prayer shelf is the chair I usually use for my daily prayer time with the Lord. Occupying center stage on the shelf is the Bible. Surrounding the Bible are a number of objects that help me focus my attention on the Lord. They serve as visual aids to remind me of the caring, concerned love of the Lord enveloping me at all times.

On the anniversary of the death of my father or mother, I place their picture on my prayer shelf to remind me to thank God for all they did for me and to praise him for giving me such good parents. When I receive such greeting cards on various occasions, I put them on my miniature altar to stimulate my prayer for the persons who sent them to me.

As I jot down these thoughts, I survey my prayer shelf to take stock of what rests on it at this moment. There is a butterfly that symbolizes the new life Jesus came to give, as he himself said, "'I came that they might have life and have it to the full'" (Jn 10:10). Next to it is a rock about the size of my fist. On the open page of the Bible I can read,

I love you, O LORD, my strength,
   O LORD, my rock, my fortress, my deliverer.
My God, my rock of refuge,
   my shield, the horn of my salvation, my strong-
      hold! (Ps 18:2-3)

The rock also reminds me that Jesus concluded the Sermon on the Mount with this thought: "'Anyone who hears my words and puts them into practice is like the wise man who built his house on rock'" (Mt 7:24).

Next week the collection on my prayer shelf could be totally different, made up of whatever comes my way.

THIRTY

Parental Prayer

"I was hungry and you gave me food." (Mt 25:35)

One of the many highlights of my life is a regular monthly meeting with a group of married couples. We come together to pray together and to share helpful hints and insights that will hopefully assist us in maturing in our spiritual life. I find this monthly meeting inspiring, supportive, and joyous.

At our last meeting we discussed the last judgment as described by Jesus and recorded by that wonderful Christian rabbi, St. Matthew, in his twenty-fifth chapter. The consensus of opinion was that Jesus was really outlining a way of life for parents. Most of the group thought Jesus was giving some comfort and reassurance to mothers and fathers as they strive to perform the demanding duties of every day in caring for their families. One person maintained that this was the surest ticket to heaven that he had ever heard of.

At this point Jim spoke up: "Let me read part of that passage again, and then we can talk about it. 'For I was hungry and you gave me food, I was thirsty and you gave me drink. I was a stranger and you welcomed me, naked and you clothed me. I was ill and you comforted me, in prison and you came to visit me'" (Mt 25:35-36).

With that we began to talk about the directives that Jesus had set forth. I cannot remember all their comments, but here are a few that come to mind.

Judy said, "I think parents have a good chance of reaching heaven, because we prepare tons of food to feed our hungry teenagers."

Steve, "Every month I wonder whether or not my salary will cover the grocery bill."

Yvonne, "Do you think that the Lord would consider changing diapers as clothing the naked?"

Damian, "Responding to that S.O.S. at night, 'I want a drink of water,' is our way of giving drink to the thirsty."

Peggy, "I also think that taking cough medicine to a sick child is an acceptable way of visiting the sick, especially at 2 a.m."

Dick, "Rescuing a little one who locked himself or

herself in the bathroom may come under the heading of visiting the imprisoned."

Debbie, "I am sure that when we babysit for someone we are taking in a stranger, as when we take in a dog or cat that 'just followed me home,' as one of the children would put it."

To all this lively discussion I could only add my amen, which translated means "right on!"

Part VI

Spring Blossoming

THIRTY-ONE

Does God Have a Favorite Color?

God looked at everything he had made, and he found it very good. (Gn 1:31)

The spring showers had stopped momentarily. Faint rays of sunshine were piercing the heavy cloud cover. I thought it safe to take a stroll down my favorite lane here in the country. As I meandered along, I was amazed at the many and varied shades of green. The whole landscape radiated and reflected green.

Each fir tree reaching heavenward had its own shade of green. The deciduous trees were still leafless, but their trunks and limbs were covered with a velvety green moss. Likewise the huge boulders, nestled under the towering trees, were heavily blanketed with moss of the most gorgeous shades. Beds of ferns dotting the landscape were waving their green fronds in the gentle breeze. Patches of grass along the lane were like a green carpet covering the bare earth. On all this greenery little drops of rain sparkled like millions of jewels. As I stood in wonder and amazement, I tried to count the various shades of green. I soon lost count, hemmed in as I was by this gorgeous array of green about me.

Green is a sign of hope. The church uses it in the liturgy to remind us that we must always have hope, regardless of what is happening in our lives. Jeremiah said it so well:

Blessed is the man who trusts in the LORD,
   whose hope is the LORD.

He is like a tree planted beside the waters
    that stretches out its roots to the stream:
It fears not the heat when it comes,
    its leaves stay green. (Jer 17:7-8)

When we place all our trust in the Lord, then we too can enkindle hope in the hearts of all who cross our path. David, the great king of Israel, praised the one who hopes in the Lord and walks in his ways. That person

  "'Is like the morning light at sunrise
    on a cloudless morning,
      making the greensward sparkle after rain.'"
  (2 Sm 23:4)

As I gazed on the sparkling panorama about me, I was convinced once again that only God could create a world of such variegated hues, tints, and shades of green. I know that God likes green, since the sacred writer informs us that "God looked at everything he had made, and he found it very good" (Gn 1:31).

As I tried to imprint this magnificent display of green on my memory, I heard myself asking, "God, is green really your favorite color?" I responded to my own question: "God, you must like green, and so do I."

THIRTY-TWO

The Legend of the Dogwood Tree

"They killed him, finally, hanging him on a tree."
                          (Acts 10:40)

My friend Fred conducted me on a tour of his extensive and elegant garden. Fred's garden is his pride and joy.

He knows every plant, tree, and shrub. He can tell you exactly the time of blooming of the perennials as well as the annuals. He waxes eloquent about any and every tree and plant. He is certainly an expert horticulturist.

As we meandered down the walk and rounded a turn, my eyes were greeted by a marvelous sight. Directly in front of us was a dogwood tree in full bloom. It resembled a huge ball of white blossoms tinged with delicate shades of red.

I gazed long and appreciatively at the exquisite beauty of this tree. When I expressed my admiration, Fred motioned me over to a bench. He asked me if I knew the legend of the dogwood tree. I had to confess that I did not. He was eager to relate it to me.

When Jesus was on earth, he said, the dogwood tree was a large, sturdy, and stately tree. Since it was so strong, it was chosen to be the tree on which Jesus was crucified. As St. Peter said, "'They killed him, finally, hanging him on a tree, only to have God raise him up on the third day'" (Acts 10:40).

The dogwood tree tried to resist being a part of this heinous crime, but all its efforts were in vain. As Jesus hung on the cross, he sensed that the tree was very distressed at being used for this shameful purpose. In his compassion, Jesus told the tree that he understood that it was being used against its will and that he appreciated its loving concern.

Jesus then promised the dogwood tree that a great change would take place. He promised the tree that it would never again grow tall enough and strong enough to be fashioned into an instrument for crucifixion. He further assured the tree that it would have an even greater beauty because of the role it had played in the redemption of the world.

At this point my friend went over and plucked a blossom from the tree, that I might observe it at close range while he continued his story. He pointed out that the blossom was shaped like a Maltese cross, with two large petals forming the vertical beam while the two shorter ones formed the cross-bar. Tenderly holding the blossom, Fred next showed me that the petals were marked with little red dots, which symbolize the nail holes in Jesus' hands and feet. The bloom has a reddish center, which symbolizes the crown of thorns.

Legends are stories that come down to us from the past. Some are popularly regarded as historical, although not verifiable. A legend can also be a source of inspiration for us.

What about the dogwood tree? Legend or not, it makes little difference to me. Since my visit with Fred, I now have a beautiful dogwood tree in my own yard. It "speaks" to me every year when it displays its gorgeous array of blossoms.

THIRTY-THREE

Do Brooks Babble?

You have visited the land and watered it. (Ps 65:10)

When I drive through the countryside, I am often tempted to stop at every stream as it wends its way through the woods or through an open field. Running water intrigues me with its beauty and charm.

One of my favorite spots is a wooded area close to home. I have found this an ideal place to be alone with the Lord in prayer. Here I enjoy his artistic creation. I usually prop myself up against a huge boulder, which towers high above me. The real attraction for this rendezvous is a little brook, which softly sings its melody as it flows along. My little brook is usually crystal clear, reflecting a diamond-like brilliance as it sparkles in the sun which streams through the trees. Some blades of grass and little flowers dip into its refreshing water as it gurgles along.

This brook reminds me of the living water that Jesus gives us. That living water is his own divine life, which he shares so generously with us. His living water flows gently through our whole being. Just as my little brook brings life and nourishment to the plants and shrubs along its path, so Jesus' living water nourishes our lives.

This stream has taught me another lesson. When the melting snows and the spring rains bring it to flood stage, it becomes murky and muddied with the debris that it has collected along its journey through the woods and fields. Its otherwise serene channel becomes cluttered with every sort of object. At this time of the year it loses much of its beauty but it is doing its duty as it noisily carries the runoff water to its destination.

This flood stage reminds me of my own life when I get involved and entangled in too many things. When this hyperactivity overtakes me, my vision, like the little brook, gets cloudy. I gather a lot of the "debris" of life and become too busy to pray, too preoccupied to listen to others, too hurried to lend a helping hand when needed.

A roaring stream cascading down a mountainside, splashing and foaming its way through a rugged channel of huge rocks, impresses me with its power. I can admire its majestic beauty, and my thoughts can soar heavenward to our Father who supplies us with this abundance of life-giving water. The effect is different from that of the quieting, soothing influence of my babbling brook.

I pray with the psalmist:

> You have visited the land and watered it;
>   greatly have you enriched it. . . .
> Thus have you prepared the land: drenching its
>   furrows,
>   breaking up its clods,
> Softening it with showers,
>   blessing its yield. (Ps 65:10-11)

To answer the question, Do brooks babble? No, they do not babble, for babbling is often unintelligible. Rather they speak ever so eloquently of the beauty, the wisdom, the power, and the providence of a loving Father who showers his goodness upon us.

THIRTY-FOUR

Rain, Now or Later

The LORD will . . . give your land rain in due season.
(Dt 28:12)

Does rain cause God a problem? I think it does. Among the many petitions flying heavenward, God hears such comments as "Yes, we need it," "Well, yes, but not now," "Remember, not too much."

The farmers fear drought and consequent crop failure, so they earnestly implore God for an abundance of rain. Their prayer pleases our loving Father very much, because he wants to be recognized as a provident God.

At the same time, those of us who are planning some outdoor activity will bombard heaven with prayers for ideal weather—that is, a nice sunny day, not too hot nor too cold.

A third group may ask for rain, but only in the amount that they deem necessary. They don't quite trust God. In his generosity he may not know just how much is enough. They fear water damage and even floods.

Still another set of petitions arise from those who realize the necessity of rain but would like to have it scheduled according to their own plans and programs. In my childhood days we used to recite a little ditty:

Rain, rain, go away.
Come again some other day.
Rain, rain, go away.
Little children want to play.

Then there are those people who dread a cloudy, overcast, rainy day because it depresses them. They know the sun is up there, but they cannot see it, and the dark day weighs heavily upon them.

The ancient Hebrews considered rain a great blessing on their parched land. In fact, they believed rain came not from the first heaven, where the sun and moon are, but from the heaven above the heavens, where God alone dwells.

A bountiful rain you showered down, O God,
    upon your inheritance;
  you restored the land when it languished;
Your flock settled in it;
  in your goodness, O God, you provided it for the
    needy. (Ps 68:10-11)

One afternoon as the rain was pelting down, it formed a little puddle on the sidewalk outside my window. I tried to count the drops as they danced in this little pool, but in vain. However, I did envision each drop as a special gift from an all-good God. So abundant are his gifts that we cannot possibly calculate them.

Moses reminds us that rain is a special blessing from the Lord. He wrote, "The LORD will open up for you his rich treasure house of the heavens, to give your land rain in due season, blessing all your undertakings, so that you will lend to many nations and borrow from none" (Dt 28:12).

As I watched the rain falling, I lapsed into the lyrics of a rather old song: "Let it rain, let it rain!"

THIRTY-FIVE

And There Was Light

"I have come to the world as its light." (Jn 12:46)

One of my favorite liturgical celebrations is the Easter Vigil, especially the procession into the church with the paschal candle. You will recall that after the lighting of the new fire, the paschal candle is lit and carried by the priest or deacon. As the procession moves toward the altar, three separate times the priest or deacon sings, "Christ, our light!" and the people respond, "Thanks be to God."

I really like this part of the celebration. Perhaps there is a human reason. Lent is over, and we are now entering into the "Alleluia" season of joy. More importantly, the occasion announces that our salvation has been won. Jesus our Redeemer has risen from the dead to seal his redemptive mission and guarantee our eternal happiness with him. Jesus not only wants to be known as the light of the world, but he also assures us that following him as the light of the world will lead us into our eternal salvation:

"I am the light of the world.
No follower of mine shall ever walk in darkness;
no, he shall possess the light of life." (Jn 8:12)

Sunshine always reminds me of the loving presence of the Lord. Just as the sun lights and sustains our world and warms and nourishes us, so the Lord's divine life warms, nurtures, sustains, and energizes us. We know that God's "sun rises on the bad and the good" and "he rains on the just and the unjust" (Mt 5:45). However, I have an option. If I want to feel the warmth of the sun and its nourishing rays, I must be receptive and cooperative. I must put myself in the sun to bask in its warmth. On the other hand, I can shut out the sun in various ways—by sitting in the shade, by closing the drapes of my room, by shutting my eyes to its light. My reactions to the sun do not change the sun at all, even if I deprive myself of its nurturing blessings.

The same is true of the divine life that Jesus wishes to pour out upon me. My reaction to his gift is extremely important to the Lord. He says:

"I have come to the world as its light,
to keep anyone who believes in me
from remaining in the dark." (Jn 12:46)

THIRTY-SIX

A Tainted Paradise

His majesty is above earth and heaven. (Ps 148:13)

It was a gorgeous spring day. The temperature was balmy, with a warm sun bathing the earth. The sky was dotted with a few fleecy clouds.

I had an appointment with my spiritual director. We decided not to waste the sunshine but to take a short drive in the country as we talked. We parked along a secondary road which led through a wooded area. It was paved and made a pleasant walking path. The name posted on this road was Paradise Lane. In many respects it was rightly dubbed, for the beauty of God seemed to envelop us as we walked along. The trees were proudly displaying their spring leaves; many of the bushes were in full bloom; a gentle breeze whispered through the trees.

My spiritual director and I were both enthralled with the beauty of nature surrounding us. We were discussing how God shares his creative power with his creatures. He created a magnificent world and asked us to bring it to an even greater stage of perfection. He endowed us with a creative ability and an intellect to seek out the secrets of his creation and to use them for our comfort, convenience, and enjoyment. We have made unique strides in science and technology—enabling us to split an atom, to orbit the earth, and even to reach other planets.

Suddenly our animated conversation extolling the goodness and beauty of God stopped. We both began to notice various objects along the roadside. Amid the beauty of God's handiwork in nature, people had strewn all sorts of debris. These discarded possessions were robbing us of the beauty God had intended us to enjoy.

Within a distance of one mile we saw a broken electric range tossed over an embankment, three large plastic bags of lawn clippings and weeds, a wheelless automobile body at the side of the road, an old refrigerator, along with a litter of cans, paper cups, and other evidence of some fast-food patrons. This is a sad commentary on our "throw-away" times. We have litter barrels of every size and description waiting to be of service. We even have attractive little bags for our vehicles. Yet these are often unused.

As I was decrying this total lack of appreciation for the beauty of our country, my companion reminded me that when we keep our focus on the Lord, life becomes brighter and more peaceful. He suggested that we keep our attention fixed on the beauty of nature and disregard the hideous litter. The psalmist expressed the same thought:

His majesty is above earth and heaven,
    and he has lifted up the horn of his people.
    (Ps 148:13-14)

Part VII

Summer Sunshine

THIRTY-SEVEN

Signs Say Something

"Know that I am with you always." (Mt 28:20)

My friend Arnie and I were taking a leisurely drive through the country on an ideal summer day. We had chosen the back roads so that we might better enjoy and appreciate the beauty of God's creation. We came upon a railroad crossing. Automatically I slowed down, and looked up and down the tracks. Arnie facetiously informed me that such caution was not necessary, since this railroad did not run according to a timetable but used an almanac instead.

The familiar "Stop, Look, and Listen" sign marked the crossing. It was rather weather-worn, but still clearly visible.

Arnie and I like to challenge each other on various topics. We also pray and reflect together sometimes, using what some may call unorthodox methods of prayer. I threw out the first bait: "What does that sign say to you? What can the Lord be saying to us through that old sign, 'Stop, Look, Listen'?"

Arnie began with the word *stop*. "I think the Lord is reminding us over and over again to stop. Stop rushing here and there; stop and set aside our business to give him some time; stop simply to rest and relax in his presence and to alert ourselves to the fact that he is with us and that he is helping us manage our lives. In the Scriptures Jesus reminds us, " 'Know that I am with you always'" (Mt 28:20). However, it is up to us to recall his presence as we race through our days. Your turn now," Arnie said.

I took the cue. "Let's pause with the second word, *look*. Today," I said to Arnie, "I think we are doing just that. As we are leisurely driving through the countryside, I have been looking. I have noticed the beauty of God's creation all around us. Just look at that big sturdy oak tree over there, waving its branches as it reaches toward heaven. Only God knows how many leaves are on that tree. It reminds me of a line from Joyce Kilmer's poem:

> " 'Poems are made by fools like me,
> But only God can make a tree.' "

I paused for a few moments as the whole panorama of God's creation lifted my spirits—the cattle grazing in the meadow, the timber-laden mountain directly in front of us, the wild flowers waving to us in the breeze. I was alone with these thoughts, and I suspected that Arnie too was engrossed in his own reflections.

Finally Arnie said, "Well, I guess it is my turn. The word *listen* speaks eloquently, doesn't it? Listening is not easy. I think very few of us listen very often. Yes, we hear a lot, but seldom do we really listen to another person. By listening I mean forgetting ourselves completely and putting ourselves in the shoes of another person.

"I do not think we can establish a good relationship with another person unless we have listened to and shared with him or her. Only then can we really get to know that person. Someplace I read that we cannot love a person we do not know, and that we cannot know a person unless we have listened to him or her."

Arnie paused for a few moments, then added rather

pensively, "I guess we cannot really know God either unless we listen to him."

Just then the shrill whistle of a train pierced the quiet atmosphere of the countryside. I just could not resist the temptation. I asked Arnie, "What was that you said back there about this railroad using an almanac instead of a timetable?"

THIRTY-EIGHT

Clouds

Sing praise . . . to our God, who covers the heavens with clouds. (Ps 147:7-8)

When we were little children, one of our favorite pastimes was to stretch out on our well-groomed lawn and watch the clouds float by. We let our imaginations run wild. We could make out an endless array of shapes and forms: from lions to lambs, from elephants to eagles, as well as horses, cows, and dogs of all types. Our vivid imaginations could discover in the clouds people of every description and dimension: young and gray-bearded, short and tall, thin and rotund, light-complexioned and swarthy.

There is still a lot of child in me when it comes to looking at clouds. I love to contemplate the white cumulus clouds against the azure blue sky or the dark heavy clouds that bring us rain. In winter the small wispy white clouds high in the atmosphere warn us that a cold spell is approaching.

One summer afternoon as I was reclining on the chaise lounge on our patio, the clouds put on a most dramatic display. Each cloud formation seemed more beautiful than the previous one, the fluffy whiteness silhouetted against the clear blue sky.

At one time in my life, heavy dark clouds spoke to me only of dampness and darkness, which brought on a feeling of depression. Then I began to realize that they were laden with moisture. These clouds are the fountains supplying drink for our sustenance and rain for our earth.

I have the impression that clouds are one of God's favorite creations. They are mentioned often in the Scriptures. In the Old Testament the Lord was present to his people under the cover of a cloud. The psalmist in his poetic way says to the Lord, "You make the clouds your chariot" (Ps 104:3). In another psalm he encourages us to sing the praises of the Lord for his infinite goodness to us:

> Sing to the LORD with thanksgiving;
>   sing praise with the harp to our God,
> Who covers the heavens with clouds,
>   who provides rain for the earth. (Ps 147:7-8)

The pillar of cloud guided the Israelites in their wanderings through the desert to the Promised Land. "The Lord preceded them, in the daytime by means of a column of cloud to show them the way, and at night by means of a column of fire to give them light" (Ex 13:21).

Without too great a stretch of the imagination, we can see clouds guiding us on our way to the Father. They may not guide us in the literal sense of the term, as a pilot car guides us along a construction site on a highway or as a radio beam keeps us on course while flying. However, as we behold and contemplate the clouds, our spirits are lifted up to our loving Father, who in his great wisdom fashioned the clouds for our enjoyment and sustenance.

THIRTY-NINE

Sprayed or Soaked?

"I came that they might have life and have it to the full."
(Jn 10:10)

I gazed in silent admiration at the huge volume of water dropping down a sheer five-hundred-foot cliff. As it fell it spread its lacy spray far and wide. Some even touched me, standing at quite a distance.

There is a legend accounting for this mighty waterfall, which I find both inspiring and heart-rending. A plague broke out among an Indian tribe living in the area. People were dying in great numbers. The medicine man insisted that the gods had to be appeased before the disease would leave them. A young maiden would have to sacrifice her life by plunging over this cliff onto the rocks below. A certain girl, after seeing her beloved and her family emaciated by the disease, volunteered to make the sacrifice.

According to the legend, when the young woman fell, an enormous spring burst forth from the rocky cliff and fell into the canyon far below. Thus the gods showed their appreciation for this sacrifice. That mighty waterfall is still cascading down the cliff today. The gods, supposedly, granted one more favor. We are told that if you observe the falling water, you will see the face of the maiden as well as the tresses of her hair in the spray. I admit I was not granted the privilege of seeing this image.

Whether or not there is any truth to this legend, it is a dim reminder of what Jesus did for us. The heroic young maiden gave her life for her people. She did so that she might bring them healing. When we were estranged from God by sin, when we were broken and wounded, Jesus sacrificed his life to redeem and heal us. He was motivated by his divine and infinite love for us. Did he not say:

"There is no greater love than this:
to lay down one's life for one's friends." (Jn 15:13)

When Jesus gave his life for our salvation, another great spiritual waterfall erupted. The immense flow of living water began and continues to cascade into our hearts. Jesus is filling us with his own divine life and love. Jesus gave us the reason for his incarnation:

"I came
that they might have life
and have it to the full." (Jn 10:10)

It would be ridiculous for me to try to catch or harness the tremendous volume of water plunging down that cliff. Even more impossible would it be to try to contain the limitless outpouring of God's love for me, since my capacity measures less than a thimbleful. How impossible it is for me to even comprehend that love! Jesus tries to explain the magnitude of his love for us:

"As the Father has loved me,
so I have loved you.
Live on in my love." (Jn 15:9)

Sitting some distance from the waterfall, I was touched only occasionally by the spray. This reminded me that unless I am willing to draw close to Jesus, I will be touched only slightly by his love. His love is always there in abundance, but if I fail to respond to him I will not be able to receive it.

Before I left, I drank a generous draft of this cool, refreshing water, reminding myself that every drop of water on our earth comes from the creative, providing love of God. The psalmist sings of this goodness of God:

> He cleft the rocks in the desert
>   and gave them water in copious floods.
> He made streams flow from the crag
>   and brought the waters forth in rivers.
>   (Ps 78:15-16)

FORTY

Hitchhikers

"I will not leave you orphaned." (Jn 14:18)

Have you ever passed up a hitchhiker along the road and really felt bad about it? Perhaps the weather was wet or cold, or the sun was blazing hot, or the hitchhiker wore a pleading expression all over his or her face—all of which intensified your guilt feelings.

Unfortunately in our times, the risk of picking up someone we do not know is too great. We know of many cases of violence inflicted on a driver and others in the car. Good judgment warns us of the danger involved.

However, valid as this reason is, I still feel a sense of guilt at times as I drive by in the comfort of my car. I try to placate this feeling by whispering a little prayer for every hitchhiker I pass. Often these persons may be poor; I ask the Lord to bless them in such a way that their poverty would have a sanctifying power in their lives. Others, I feel, are running from reality and chasing dreams; they too need my prayers.

I ask Jesus to accompany each person, as he accompanied the two disciples on the road to Emmaus. As Jesus explained the Scriptures to these disciples, he kept their hearts burning within them. I ask Jesus to bring all hitchhikers his peace and joy in spite of their hardships.

We could think of Jesus himself as a kind of hitchhiker. He traveled the length and breadth of the Holy Land to proclaim the good news to anyone who would listen. He experienced fatigue, as John relates: "Jesus, tired from his journey, sat down at the well" (Jn 4:6).

Jesus hitched a ride on another person's donkey when he made his triumphal entry into Jerusalem on Palm Sunday. Often Jesus did not know where he was going to stay. He probably slept under the stars many nights, for he says, " 'The foxes have lairs, the birds in the sky have nests, but the Son of Man has nowhere to lay his head' " (Mt 8:20).

Philip too was a hitchhiker who brought a blessing to the person who offered him a ride (see Acts 8:26-40). He was instructed by an angel to " 'head south toward the road which goes from Jerusalem to Gaza.' " As he did so, a court official from Ethiopia was riding along in his carriage, reading the prophet Isaiah. When Philip caught up to the carriage, the official invited him "to get in and sit down beside him" to explain the word of God. This incident had a happy ending. The official received the gift of faith and was baptized.

I often remind myself that I too am a hitchhiker through this land of exile on my way to heaven. At s my journey becomes wearisome, my baggage r heavy, the miles long, and the grade steep. How grateful I am when a brother or sister comes along to assist me and encourage me, or better still, to walk a few miles with me.

When the way becomes difficult, I need to remember that Jesus said:

"I will not leave you orphaned;
I will come back to you." (Jn 14:18)

In his final commission and instruction to us Jesus reminds us once again: "'Know that I am with you always, until the end of the world!'" (Mt 28:20).

FORTY-ONE

Walking and Talking

"I will dwell with them and walk among them.'"
(2 Cor 6:16)

Jim is my neighbor and also my friend. G.K. Chesterton would call that an anomaly, for he said, "The Bible tells us to love our neighbor, and it also tells us to love our enemies. Well, of course, they are the same people." Not so with Jim. We have become friendly neighbors and neighborly friends, even though our companionship is mostly limited to occasional walks together.

Some years ago Jim suffered a heart attack. After he recovered, he was strongly advised to take a walk each day. He is faithful in doing so. During his solitary walks Jim does a lot of reflecting. When opportunity permits, I walk with him. Together we can settle all the world's problems, but unfortunately no one asks for our solutions.

Jim is convinced of the value of walking as exercise.

One day as we walked along, he began philosophizing on the value and necessity of walking. He maintains that walking does more for a person than any other kind of exercise. It has many bonus fruits. Walking will lift your spirits, even if you are not down that day, Jim said. It enables you to expel poisons from your body caused by tension and anxieties. God's oxygen purifies your lungs and blood and invigorates you. Jim went on to say that when he meets someone during a walk, stranger or acquaintance, he breathes a little prayer for that person.

Walking in the fresh air gives one a sense of belonging to this vast world of ours. Think of the thousands of miles a person can walk and still cover only a little patch of our planet. With a sweeping gesture Jim said, "Look at the sky—that space bewilders me. Being surrounded by the immensity and beauty of God's creation fills me with a sense of awe and wonder, of reverence and humility."

After this statement, Jim and I walked along in silence, alone with our own thoughts. After some time I told him that I like to walk at different times of the day and also in different places. In the early morning I enjoy the stillness, when I can listen more attentively to the chirping of the birds. I also hear some distant sounds which seem drowned out at other times of the day. A special time for me to walk is at night, under the immense canopy of stars and galaxies. Then the only sound is perhaps the hoot of an owl or the drone of an airplane.

I also told Jim that walking down a busy street is always an experience for me. I see people who can walk only at a slow pace, some limping along quite painfully. A lot of people walk rather rapidly and seem to be oblivious of anyone else.

I reminded Jim that we were like the two disciples going to Emmaus. Although the Lord did not appear to us as he did to the disciples, I felt that he was really with us, especially when Jim pointed out God's presence and power in all of creation. After all, the Lord promised:

"I will dwell with them and walk among them.
I will be their God
and they shall be my people." (2 Cor 6:16)

Part VIII

Golden Autumn

FORTY-TWO

In the Shade of a Pine Tree

"If the grain of wheat dies, it produces much fruit."
(Jn 12:24)

When I visit Peter, we often sit in the shade of a large ponderosa pine in his back yard. Peter is retired, and he likes to philosophize with me, as he puts it.

We were recently enjoying a visit when a large pine cone fell from the tree and bounced toward Peter's feet. This was his cue to begin his discourse.

"Take a look at this dried-up pine cone," he said. "What does it say to you? Its exterior is rough and prickly. These once pollen-rich scales are now spread wide open and empty.

"Just reflect momentarily on the function of this pine cone. As it matured on the tree, the winged seed enclosed in it began to ripen. When the seed had matured, the scales opened and sent the seed off on a gentle breeze. The cone gave up its seed and sent it forth to find a suitable environment where it could plant itself and grow into a mighty tree, just like this one shading us now."

As I listened attentively, Peter was encouraged to go on. "You and I are like a pine cone, meaning no disrespect to you or the Creator. Like the pine cone, we are expected to produce some good fruit and let that fruit extend far and wide to reach many different people. Perhaps the good we do might help them. It might encourage them, bring them some hope, and give them some inspiration. It could, even like the seed from the pine cone, give them a new start in life, to grow and mature into something worthwhile like a big tree.

"There is one catch to it, however." Peter was almost soliloquizing now, as if reminding himself. "We've got to be able to give up what we produced in order to give the new seed a chance to find its own home and grow.

"It's very much like what parents have to do. They must nurture their children, train them, educate them, love them, and then let them fly from the nest to begin a new life. That's what I had to do with all six of mine, and it wasn't easy, especially after their mother died and I was left alone with them. They were all I had in this world." There was a long pause.

Finally I interjected, "I believe that is what Jesus was talking about when he used the example of the grain of wheat. Remember when he said:

> "'Unless the grain of wheat falls to the earth and
>   dies,
> it remains just a grain of wheat.
> But if it dies,
> it produces much fruit.'" (Jn 12:24)

I was obvious that Peter wanted to be alone with his reflections and reveries. As I excused myself, he said, "Just call me Old Pine Cone Pete."

FORTY-THREE

Candlelight

"Your light must shine before men." (Mt 5:16)

I had the good fortune to lead a day of prayer for the staff of a parochial school before the beginning of the scholastic year. It turned out to be a memorable day for me. I was inspired by the sincerity of all those present, especially by their prayerful approach to their responsibilities for the coming year.

The closing ceremony was very impressive. It consisted of commissioning each person for the assignment they had accepted for that year. Arranged on a table was a huge cluster of flickering candles. No two candles were alike. Some were short and some tall; others were square and still others round. Each candle had its own special color and hue. I had never seen such an array of candles nor such a rainbow of colors.

After each staff member was commissioned for his or her special assignment, they were to select a candle. This was to remind them of the task they had assumed for the coming year.

The principal of the school had explained to me that just as each candle was different, so each person is endowed with different gifts and talents. Each staff member is expected to use his or her gifts for the good of all the pupils and for the success of the whole educational program in the parish.

Candles have a long history. Not too many generations ago they were the main source of illumination in our homes. They were also used in our churches so that the celebrant could read the text of the liturgical books.

Today candles serve mostly decorative purposes. Their many sizes, shapes, forms, and colors enhance the decor of our homes. They add beauty to a room when they are strategically arranged. We enjoy eating and visiting by candlelight. Watching their restless flames helps us relax.

The vast variety of candles makes them appropriate gifts for many different occasions. They can be molded into a diversity of shapes—from Santa Claus to saints, from angels to animals, from buildings to birds.

A friend gave me a candle that is shaped like an owl. An inscription came with it: "If you study by the light of this candle, you will become as wise as this old bird." I have another candle that is a statue of a saint. I like to think that if my life is consumed in the service of the Lord as this saint's was, then I have it made.

Candles are sacred and symbolic. In the liturgy of the church they represent the presence of Christ, the light of the world. As a candle burns, it is totally consumed. As I watch the flickering of a candle, I am reminded that my life too must be spent in the service of the Lord and my neighbor. Didn't Jesus say, " 'You are the light of the world. . . . Your light must shine before men so that they may see goodness in your acts and give praise to your heavenly Father' " (Mt 5:14, 16)?

My life of dedication, my loving concern for others, my spirit of joy, should light up the world around me. When I light up my little world, that same light will illumine my life also.

FORTY-FOUR

The Symbol of Triumph

"So must the Son of Man be lifted up." (Jn 3:14)

One autumn afternoon I was traveling to a little town some hundred miles away. Coming around a curve just a few miles from my destination, I was greeted with a gorgeous panoramic view. In a magnificent valley hemmed in by high timber-decked mountains lay the little town. Since I was ahead of schedule, I pulled off the road in order to enjoy this beautiful scene.

Towering over the dwellings below was the spire of

a church, dominated by a cross. The cross seemed to be keeping vigil over the people living in its shadow. The cross is such a telling symbol. Its vertical shaft joins earth to heaven, while its horizontal beam embraces the world. It is a universal symbol. Our Christian institutions, churches, schools, and hospitals are usually adorned with an imposing cross.

We display the cross in many other ways. It has become a popular piece of jewelry in a variety of forms and materials. A cross or crucifix worn by someone is a sign of dedication to a Christian way of life, often a vowed life.

We usually begin our prayers by tracing the sign of the cross on ourselves. We bless ourselves and others with the sign of the cross. Religious objects are blessed with the sign of the cross.

The sign of the cross is used extensively when administering the sacraments. How often we have been absolved with the sign of the cross. In the eucharistic celebration it occurs frequently.

The cross is such a sacred symbol not only because it reminds us of our own sinfulness and our need for redemption; even more importantly, it speaks to us of the redeeming love of Jesus poured out for every one of us.

In every cross we can read the message of divine love. Jesus said:

"There is no greater love than this:
to lay down one's life for one's friends." (Jn 15:13)

On other occasions Jesus foretold the magnetic power that the cross would have in our lives:

"Just as Moses lifted up the serpent in the desert,
so must the Son of Man be lifted up." (Jn 3:14)

As the time of his being "lifted up" came closer, he said once again:

"I—once I am lifted up from earth—
will draw all men to myself." (Jn 12:32)

After reflecting for some time, I drove into the village to greet the pastor before taking care of the business for which I had come. I shared with him my experience on the road. He responded, "How gracious is the Lord, for today happens to be the feast of the Triumph of the Cross."

Surely the cross of Jesus has triumphed and will continue to triumph.

FORTY-FIVE

Through the Fog

"There is your mother." (Jn 19:27)

All the passengers were aboard the airplane, but we still sat at the gate for a considerable time. Finally we moved out to the end of the runway. There we sat for at least an hour, motors purring, eager for a takeoff.

The cause of the delay was the weather. A dense fog had settled over the airport that morning, delaying all flights. The crew and the air controllers in the tower were confident that it would lift or burn off at any moment.

Fog brings back to me a special memory from my childhood. My mother and I were walking to church for the early Mass one Sunday. The fog was so dense that I could see only a few feet in front of me. I was petrified. I feared that I might run into someone or something, that I might trip and fall, or even worse, that I might lose my way. I clung to my mother's hand with a vise-like grip. She lovingly reassured me, and together we braved the fog and arrived safely at church in time for Mass.

Through the years I have many times thought about that morning in the fog. I think of it especially when my life seems to be shrouded in a fog. At times I cannot see clearly the direction in which the Lord is calling, nor does he make the solution to a weighty problem evident. I sometimes grope about, wary and fearful of what might lie ahead.

At times like these I need to remind myself that I may not be able to see far ahead, but I do have the assurance that the Lord is with me. Just as he accompanied the disciples on the road to Emmaus, so he is with me. Did he not say, "'Know that I am with you always, until the end of the world'" (Mt 28:20)?

I often think about Mary our Mother. She did not fully understand God's plan of salvation for her life, nor did she clearly see her specific role. Each day she had to step out in faith. She placed her trust in the Lord. Each day she had to renew her commitment to the Lord.

Just as my own mother grasped my hand and guided me on that memorable foggy morning, so Mary is with me always. This is what Jesus meant when, from his deathbed on the cross, he gave us his mother: "'There is your mother'" (Jn 19:27).

How does Mary guide us? Her directive to us in quite clear and compelling: "'Do whatever he tells you'" (Jn 2:5).

I was roused from my reverie by the voice of the captain announcing, "We have been cleared for take-off. Flight attendants, please take your seats."

In a few moments we were racing and roaring down the runway and into our flight.

FORTY-SIX

Meditation in Motion

God looked at everything he had made, and he found it very good. (Gn 1:31)

My niece Lois delights in taking her old uncle on hikes through open fields and wooded areas. Needless to say, it doesn't require much convincing, since walking is one of my favorite exercises, especially when it's through the countryside.

On one such outing we found a trail through a thickly wooded area, traversing the hills and valleys. For some time we talked and walked along, enjoying each other's company to the accompaniment of the wind whispering through the trees and the rustling of leaves underfoot. It was delightful.

When we came to an intersecting trail, Lois suggested that we walk alone on different trails, in order to reflect in silence and to enjoy the scenery alone with the Lord. This proved to be a gratifying experience.

A whole new world unfolds before me when I walk contemplatively. By a contemplative walk I mean a slow-paced, meditative sauntering along. This type of walk gives me ample time for many things: to admire the exquisite beauty of a flower, which might otherwise receive only a casual glance; to gaze in wonder at an insect crossing my path, carrying a burden twice its size; to hear a squirrel bickering at me because I invaded his domain; to listen to the song of a bird; to hear a barking dog tell me, "Hi, there! Have a good walk. Wish I could go with you"; to observe a perfectly symmetrical tree lifting its leafy branches heavenward; to inhale the pine-scented aroma that lingers in the air;

to feel the velvety softness of the meadow grass spreading a carpet before me.

My external senses act as antennae to transfer these experiences into the depth of my soul. There I can know them as God experiences, and I can see the divine in the mundane about me.

On this particular walk I soon became lost in the wonder of God's creation and his loving care and concern for all that he had made. As the inspired writer said, "God looked at everything he had made, and he found it very good" (Gn 1:31).

As I sat on a log totally absorbed with these reflections and oblivious of my surroundings, two loving arms caught me in a warm embrace. Lois exclaimed, "Isn't God wonderful!"

Yes, Lord, I thank you for family and friends, especially for this beautiful niece of mine who loves you so dearly.

Part IX

Winter Wonderland

FORTY-SEVEN

God Must Like Snow

He spreads snow like wool. (Ps 147:16)

God must take a special delight in the white fluffy blankets of snow he sends our way. Its brilliance creates a winter wonderland. It covers everything with its sparkling beauty.

God must take pleasure too in seeing his children frolic in the snow. We enjoy a whole variety of winter sports: there is sledding down hills and embankments; for others the ponds and lakes provide skating; the more adventurous enjoy the ski slopes; and in our technological age we can race over the countryside in snowmobiles.

Snow also challenges a person's artistic talent. In addition to the traditional snowman, elaborate snow sculptures appear, weather permitting.

The ancient Hebrews considered rain so vitally important to their survival that they believed it came only from the second heaven, where God lives far above the first heaven. I was curious to see if the inspired writers said anything about snow. Sirach gives us a beautiful account of a wintry condition:

He sprinkles the snow like fluttering birds;
   it comes to settle like swarms of locusts.
Its shining whiteness blinds the eyes,
   the mind is baffled by its steady fall.
He scatters frost like so much salt;
   it shines like blossoms on the thornbush.

Cold northern blasts he sends
    that turn the ponds to lumps of ice.
He freezes over every body of water,
    and clothes each pool with a coat of mail.
(Sir 43:18-21)

The prophet uses the image of snow to assure us of God's infinite mercy and compassion in forgiving our sinfulness:

Though your sins be like scarlet,
    they may become white as snow;
Though they be crimson red,
    they may become white as wool. (Is 1:18)

David uses a similar metaphor when he prays for forgiveness:

Cleanse me of sin with hyssop, that I may be purified;
    wash me, and I shall be whiter than snow.
(Ps 51:9)

Elsewhere the psalmist proclaims God's power and providence in sending his gift of snow:

He spreads snow like wool;
    frost he strews like ashes.
He scatters his hail like crumbs;
    before his cold the waters freeze.
He sends his word and melts them;
    he lets his breeze blow and the waters run.
(Ps 147:16-18)

It is surprising how frequently the Scriptures use the image of snow, especially since the climate of Israel is semi-tropical. As we can see from these few quotes, snow was considered a special blessing from the Lord. In our times it is still a marvelous gift of God for our enjoyment and for many other blessings. We too can say:

Ice and snow, bless the Lord;
    praise and exalt him above all forever. (Dn 3:70)

FORTY-EIGHT

Frosty Lace

Who gives the hoarfrost its birth in the skies . . . ? (Jb 38:29)

When I arose one wintry morning and opened my drapes, I was greeted with a gorgeous scene. During the night the Lord had decorated all the trees and bushes with a fine, silky hoarfrost, creating a winter wonderland of dainty lace that no human hand could have designed. Each pattern was artistically done, each one different, each one beautiful.

This magnificent scene must reflect in some small way the exquisite beauty of our loving Father. How happy God must be to delight his creatures with indescribable wonder such as this! The Lord hinted at the beauty and power of his creation when he asked Job, "Who gives the hoarfrost its birth in the skies . . . ?" (Jb 38:29).

When the Israelites were starving in the desert after their miraculous release from the slavery of Egypt, God promised to feed them with the bread from heaven. Moses attempted to describe the daily manna in the desert: "There on the surface of the desert were fine flakes like hoarfrost on the ground" (Ex 16:14).

Just as God fed the hungry Israelites, so he inspires our hearts and minds with the beauty of his loving care in displaying such beauty.

As I stood at my window rapt in the scene, the first rays of the morning sun appeared on the horizon. This light set the hoarfrost aglow, making it sparkle like thousands of diamonds. Even as I feasted on this brilliance, I became aware that the warmth of the sun would soon rob us of this heavenly beauty and transform the whole scene.

I was reminded of how Joshua asked the sun and moon to stand still until the Israelites had gained a victory. The result of his prayer was that "the sun halted in the middle of the sky; not for a whole day did it resume its swift course" (Jos 10:13).

Since I dared not ask for such a miraculous favor, I begged the Lord to imprint the beauty of this scene on my mind. I could then concur with the author of the Book of Joshua: "Never before or since was there a day like this, when the LORD obeyed the voice of a man" (Jos 10:14).

FORTY-NINE

Clearing a Path

"Make ready the way of the Lord.'" (Lk 3:4)

It was Thursday, and it was my turn to host our weekly prayer group. All day the sun shone brightly on the snow. Then, in the late afternoon, big feather-like flakes began fluttering to earth.

When the snow stopped, I immediately began shoveling off the walkway. I think of a clear walk not only as a safety precaution but also as a welcome mat for guests as they arrive. Shoveling snow can be a chore, especially if the snow comes at an inconvenient time. But as I shoveled, my thoughts centered on the oft-repeated words of John the Baptist as he pleaded with his hearers to prepare for the coming of the Lord:

> "'Make ready the way of the Lord,
> Clear him a straight path.'" (Lk 3:4)

The people of John's day understood this urgent message. At that time, when a king or some other important personage made a tour of the country, a courier was sent ahead to advise the people to prepare a way for him by clearing the narrow roadway and leveling the gullies.

In my own way I was preparing for the coming of the Lord in my friends, whom I expected to arrive momentarily. Jesus assures us that he is present in our midst: "'Where two or three are gathered in my name, there am I in their midst'" (Mt 18:20).

John the Baptist used his admonition in a spiritual sense. He urges us to prepare for the coming of the Lord by freeing ourselves of any attachments that would prevent the Lord from transforming us into the kind of person he wants us to be. Just as we have to be prepared to clear away the snow each time it falls, so we must be constantly on the alert to rid ourselves of any obstacle that would prevent the Lord from working freely in us. The Baptist also encourages us to be open and receptive to God's love and to respond generously to his love. It was a very prayerful evening for our little cluster. I think all of us felt the presence of the Lord in our midst. By the way, it did not snow anymore that evening.

Perhaps I should send a message to John the Baptist that I did try to make ready the way of the Lord and I did clear a path for him. However, it was not a straight one, since my walkway is laid out in a wide curve.

They tell me that snowblowers are wonderful labor-saving machines. Wish I had one!

FIFTY

A Blanket of Blessing

From the heavens the rain and snow come down. (Is 55:10)

I sat by my window and watched the huge flakes of snow gently fluttering down. Hours of this weather had already formed a magnificent white blanket of several inches. The ground, the trees, and the bushes all seemed to welcome its comforting warmth. No artist could fully capture this landscape in all its glory and beauty.

Snow is such a blessing. It protects plants and trees from bitter cold, which could cause severe damage. When it melts, its moisture nourishes the land. The frost and snow renew and refresh Mother Earth, preparing it for another bountiful harvest.

We seem to pass through a similar cycle. As twilight fades into the darkness of night, we go to rest under the blanket of God's love to be renewed and refreshed and strengthened for another day. As the earth arises new and refurbished every spring, so each morning we too arise rested and renewed for another day in the service of the Lord and all those he sends into our lives.

We are also renewed through the powerful word of God. His word can transform us into the kind of person he wants us to be. His word inspires and motivates us to tackle the demanding duties of each day. His word can create and recreate good wholesome attitudes of mind and heart within us. The time we spend in listening to his word and permitting it to find a home in our heart can rightly be called our attitudinal adjustment hour.

The prophet Isaiah captured this image of the rain and snow providing a rich harvest and compared it to the power of the word of God:

> For just as from the heavens
>   the rain and snow come down
> And do not return there
>   till they have watered the earth,
>   making it fertile and fruitful,
> Giving seed to him who sows
>   and bread to him who eats,
> So shall my word be
>   that goes forth from my mouth;
> It shall not return to me void,
>   but shall do my will,
>   achieving the end for which I sent it. (Is 55:10-11)

I was riveted to the window, reflecting on the infinite wisdom and goodness of the Lord. I resolved that I would never again complain about the inconveniences that snow causes me from time to time. What difference does it make if I have to shovel a sidewalk or if I find driving difficult? The marvelous blanket of God's goodness covering our needy earth is a welcome blessing.

FIFTY-ONE

One Snowflake

What is man that you should be mindful of him. . . ?
(Ps 8:5)

Did you ever catch a snowflake on your sleeve and gaze in awe at its artistry? Its delicate, intricate, lacy form is a beauty to behold. If you were to catch a second and a third one, you would discover that they are all very different and yet so indescribably beautiful.

Studying a snowflake can easily lead to a meditative mood. Even a casual reflection can fill us with wonder and awe. God's creative genius is displayed in each individual snowflake. Snowflakes are one of the myriad and miraculous works of God's creative love. As they accumulate on the ground, they sparkle like a million diamonds.

Snowflakes can remind us of the goodness of God in creating each of us in his own image and likeness. In fact, we are the masterpieces of his creation. As creatures we too, like the snowflakes, must radiate God's goodness and beauty. At times it may seem hard to see the beauty in another person, but as the snowflake's beauty and intricacy is brought out all the more when it is seen against a dark background, so we must behold another person against the background of God's creative love.

As we recognize the goodness and kindness of God in creating the human race, we may be moved to pray with the psalmist:

> When I behold your heavens, the works of your
>   fingers,
>   the moon and the stars which you set in place—
> What is man that you should be mindful of him,
>   or the son of man that you should care for him?
>   (Ps 8:4-5)

A snowflake on our sleeve soon melts. However, before its beauty fades, it has brought joy and wonder to our heart. The fate of the snowflake can bring to mind the brevity of our own life on earth. Just as snowflakes flutter to earth for our enjoyment and to water and nourish the earth, so our lives have two specific purposes: to radiate God's beauty and to accomplish the work he asks of us. Then the Lord is delighted to welcome us into the exquisite beauty of his presence, to praise and glorify him forever and ever.

When a newly elected pope is being crowned and enthroned, he is visually reminded of the transitory nature of this life on earth. A bit of flammable material blazes up and burns out quickly. During this brief ceremony the pope hears, *Sic transit gloria mundi*, "So passes the glory of this world."

The snowflake does the same for us as it melts away. This is not a negative reminder, but a recalling of the greater glory that awaits us after we have finished our work on earth. The Scottish poet Robert Burns says it so well:

> But pleasures are like poppies spread;
> You seize the flower, its bloom is shed;
> Or like the snow falls in the river
> a moment white—then it melts forever.

Finale

FIFTY-TWO

Stay Awake

It is now the hour for you to wake from sleep. (Rom 13:11)

In one of his power-packed allocutions, Martin Luther King, Jr. said that some people die at the age of forty but keep on breathing until they are eighty. I think the truth expressed in this statement can also be applied to our spiritual growth.

We can easily become so engrossed with the mundane around us that we fail to recognize the divine contained in it. Our lives are charged with the divine, but we are not always aware of the presence and power of God in our environment.

Just as the sunshine on a beautiful summer day warms and nourishes us, so God's love is being poured out upon us at every moment of our existence. This figure of speech is weak, since sunshine can hardly compare with the fathomless, unconditional love of God constantly enveloping us.

Staying alert to God's abiding presence is a continuing process. Keeping ourselves aware of his love requires an ongoing effort. We can never be too alert to his presence, power, and beauty in our lives. In the Garden of Gethsemane Jesus pleaded with his disciples, "'Remain here and stay awake.'" When they failed him, he registered his disappointment: "'So you could not stay awake with me for even an hour?'" (Mt 26:38, 40). Jesus was disappointed not only because he missed the comfort and consolation their prayer support would have given him, but even more because they were not aware of the tremendous love he had for them, a love that would cost him his life. The Lord begs us in a similar way to look beyond the mundane around us. He wants us to stay awake, to be alert, to be aware, to experience his dynamic presence and power in our midst. He would advise us to be aware of the gift of his invigorating oxygen, which we inhale twenty-five thousand times each day; to be grateful for the gift of sight enabling us to read this printed page; to stay awake to behold the beauty of his creative love surrounding us; to be alert to enjoy his personal protection and guidance throughout each day; to be aware of the new life budding forth from a germinating seed; to see the busy bee pollinating our fruits and flowers.

The list could go on endlessly. This is what I mean by perceiving the "mystery in the mundane." The sacred writer advises us to do the same: "Take care to do all these things, for you know the time in which we are living. It is now the hour for you to wake from sleep, for our salvation is closer than when we first accepted the faith" (Rom 13:11).